RETIRE *With* CONFIDENCE

RETIRE *With* CONFIDENCE

52 Questions to Ask Before You Retire—WITH EXPERT ANSWERS

The WORRY-FREE RETIREMENT Series

Randy L. Thurman
CFP®, CPA/PFS™

Advantage | Books

Published by Advantage Books, Charleston, South Carolina.
An imprint of Advantage Media.

Printed in the United States of America.

10 9 8 7 6 5 4 3 2 1

ISBN: 979-8-89188-389-5 (Paperback)
ISBN: 979-8-89188-390-1 (eBook)

Library of Congress Control Number: 2026900328

Cover design by Lance Buckley.
Layout design by Ruthie Wood.

Advantage Books is an imprint of Advantage Media Group. Advantage Media helps busy entrepreneurs, CEOs, and leaders write and publish a book to grow their business and become the authority in their field. Advantage authors comprise an exclusive community of industry professionals, idea-makers, and thought leaders. For more information go to advantagemedia.com.

02-19-2026 4:25

For Dad …

You taught me that "it don't take long to live a lifetime,"

words I only truly understood after you were gone.

In the embers of your wisdom, I found my path.

In my own son's eyes, I see your fire burning still.

This book—and generations to come—carry your fingerprints.

Contents

Author's Note

This book is for educational and informational purposes only and is not intended to provide assurances or guarantees of success; neither do the strategies contained herein represent personal recommendations for any reader. The reader is encouraged to consult a competent financial advisor to address their individual needs.

Statements and references in this book should in no way be construed as endorsements or recommendations of the services of any investment advisor and/or brokerage company. Any given investment advisor and/or brokerage company is solely responsible for its services.

Links to resources and services are provided solely for the reader's convenience, and their inclusion herein should not be considered an endorsement of any resources, services, or products.

Information in this book has been obtained from sources deemed to be reliable, but neither the author nor the publisher warrants or guarantees the timeliness or accuracy of this information, nor shall they be liable for any errors or inaccuracies, regardless of cause. The information is believed to be factual and up-to-date, but it should not be regarded as a complete analysis of the subject. The recommendations and opinions stated herein are subject to change without notice.

Information in this book is not an offer to buy or sell, nor a solicitation of any offer to buy or sell, any securities mentioned.

Past performance may not be indicative of future results; therefore, the reader should not assume that future performance of any specific investment or strategy will be profitable or that it will perform similarly in the future.

Different investment types carry different kinds of risk; therefore, it should be noted that any specific investment or class of investment may or may not be suitable for any particular person or portfolio.

Historical performance of investment indexes and classes generally does not reflect the deduction of transaction or advisory fees and/or custodial charges, which decrease overall performance. Economic factors, market conditions, and investment strategies impact every portfolio and may result in a portfolio that does not match a particular benchmark.

Preface

After four decades as a financial advisor specializing in retirement planning, I've found that the path to a confident retirement is paved with questions. Some are straightforward, others complex, and all deserving of thoughtful answers built on experience and expertise.

My journey in writing *Retire with Confidence* began during a client appreciation event several years ago. As I looked around the room at the faces of clients I've guided through this major life transition, I realized that, despite their diverse backgrounds, most had initially arrived at my office asking remarkably similar questions. A pattern emerged across thousands of pre-retirement consultations; the same core concerns, uncertainties, and hopes appeared consistently, regardless of net worth or background.

I recall meeting with Robert and Sarah, a couple in their early sixties who came to my office clutching a folder of retirement calculations they'd done themselves. Despite their diligent planning, they were paralyzed by uncertainty. "How do we know if this is enough?" Sarah asked. "What about healthcare costs? What if the market crashes right after we retire?" Their questions cascaded one after another. Three meetings later, with a clear plan in place, Robert shared, with teary eyes, "For the first time, I feel I can actually look forward to my retirement day instead of dreading it."

Then there was Michael, a successful business owner who had accumulated significant wealth but had no idea how to structure it for retirement income. "I know how to make money," he told me, "but I don't know how to make it last." His question—how he could transform a lifetime of savings into sustainable retirement income—is one I've answered hundreds of times, each with personalized nuance.

These experiences inspired my previous books *The All-Weather Retirement Portfolio* and *Five Steps to Finding a Financial Advisor You Can Trust*. But even after those publications, the questions kept coming. And so I began documenting the most common and consequential questions that potential retirees asked, eventually collecting the 52 that are included in this book.

Retire with Confidence is designed to address the questions that keep pre-retirees awake at night. It provides clear, actionable answers based not on theory but on four decades of guiding real people through their retirement transitions. Each question in this book is answered with the same care and attention I would give if you were sitting in my office.

My purpose in writing this book is simple: to bring peace of mind to what should be one of life's most fulfilling transitions. Too many people approach retirement with anxiety rather than anticipation. By addressing these 52 essential questions, I hope to transform your uncertainty into confidence, your fears into comfort.

So, how can you best use this book? Think of it as your retirement road trip planning guide. The structure is designed to lead you on a well-planned journey, starting with those fundamental "Am I ready?" questions, like checking your fuel gauge and tire pressure to make sure your vehicle is in shape for the trip (chapters 1 and 2). Then, you'll map out your various income streams to know what rest areas and gas stations are available to fuel your retirement adventures and help you plan how far you can travel (chapters 3 through 6). Next, this guide will describe all the investment and tax strategies, threats, and hazards to keep you on track and out of harm's way, even when you hit those unexpected detours or your GPS points you toward a "shortcut" that really leads over a cliff (chapters 7 through 9). Finally, for those who prefer to share the driving, there's advice on how to hire a good copilot (chapter 10).

With this book, you can read from start to finish, choosing to drive the scenic route, or you can skip around from question to question, taking the express lane straight to whatever destination is currently calling out to you. Sometimes you'll want the full cross-country adventure, and sometimes you'll just need to know the fastest route to get unstuck from whatever jam you're in right now. Whether you read this book cover to cover or flip to the questions most relevant to your situation, my goal is for you to set it down thinking, "Now I understand. Now I can move forward."

With gratitude for allowing me to share this journey with you,

Randy L. Thurman

Chapter 1

Am I Ready to Retire?

"Dave was only retired for six months before he wanted to go back to work," said Joan, the wife of a couple I was advising.[1] They had plenty of retirement savings and no longer needed more earned income, but it turns out that Dave missed doing something productive with his time. His honey do list, check; all the projects he'd put off, check; visiting family and friends he hadn't seen in a while, check; taking that long-awaited vacation to Tahiti, check. Now, on most days, he no longer had "a reason to get up each morning," said Joan. It was stressing him—and her—out, his doing nothing. Dave just wasn't emotionally ready to retire. So, he ended up taking a semi-volunteer job, working three days a week at a wage "lower than he's worth," and now he's happy as can be.

As you approach the golden years of your life, the idea of retirement is probably becoming more and more enticing. You may be looking forward to relaxing days spent enjoying your favorite activities, quality

---

1 Dave and Joan and all the names in this book are not the actual names of my clients. And, in some cases, I've changed or combined facts from real-life scenarios in order to illustrate common situations I've encountered over the years.

time with loved ones, and travel adventures near and far—all free from the requirement of earning a living. As my clients near retirement, I advise them to ask themselves two basic questions: Are they financially ready to retire, *and* are they emotionally ready to retire? You've probably already been asking yourself the first question—whether you have enough money to retire—and are now looking for some advice. Maybe that's even why you opened this book. But have you asked yourself the second question—or maybe not so much? In my experience, it's critical to ask them both, so that's where we'll start …

Question 1: Am I emotionally ready to retire?

This should actually be the first question that everyone asks, but almost nobody does. I see it all too often. Many who reach retirement age will answer, "After all my years of hard work, you'd better believe I'm ready!" Don't be so sure.

> This should be the first question that everyone asks, but almost nobody does.

Maybe your financial numbers look good, but determining whether you are emotionally ready to retire involves a completely different set of calculations. Here are some factors to think about and work through for yourself:

- **Identity and purpose.** For many, work provides a sense of identity and purpose, even though you might not think so at first. So how will you find fulfillment in retirement? Perhaps hobbies, a sport (pickleball is my favorite!), or volunteer opportunities can provide some sense of purpose. You may even realize that you're not quite ready to retire from work you love. Think about it for yourself.

- **Social connections.** Evaluate your current social network at and away from work. Retirement can lead to a loss of the social interactions that came along with your job. How will you maintain connections—or build new ones—in retirement?

- **The stress of change.** Retirement is a change, and change, even for the better, is often stressful. I remember reading an article about quantifying life events and the stress they can cause, with all the different events measured in "life change units." Retirement was in the top ten, not far behind events such as the death of a family member, divorce, imprisonment, personal injury … things like that. Retirement involves a big change. Most of your routine and structure will disappear. Do you understand the magnitude of the change you're about to face, and are you prepared for the impact?

Do you understand the magnitude of the change you're about to face, and are you prepared for the impact?

- **Partner relationships.** The wife of one retired client said to me only half-jokingly, "Now I have twice the husband but half the income." If you have a partner, retirement doesn't impact just your own life; it impacts your partner in a big way, too. Discuss expectations with your spouse. How much time will you spend together and apart (and how)? How will you spend your "entertainment" money? What does retirement look like to you? To your spouse?

- **Health and activity level.** Health and keeping active are such important and often neglected aspects of retirement planning. How are you going to maintain (or improve!) your physical health? (Did I mention pickleball?) When you're healthy and active, you'll sleep better, feel better, and enjoy an overall better quality of life.

- **The bucket list.** What do you want to do in retirement—places to see, things to learn, projects to complete, etc.? Now is a great time to sit down and reflect on what you want to do in retirement. Then write down your list and get ready to start checking them off! (And if you're married, as I mentioned above, be sure to compare notes with your spouse.)
- **Your legacy.** What do you want to hand down or leave behind? Your retirement years are a time to cement your legacy—whether it's through mentoring, giving back to your community, or passing on something that's uniquely you.
- **Trial retirement.** If possible, consider taking an extended vacation or a sabbatical from your job even before you're ready to retire. This can give you a taste of what full-time retirement might feel like.

Have you thought about many of these issues? You can't necessarily answer all these questions right now, but taking some time to reflect can be really beneficial and thought-provoking—and also help to illuminate some potential blind spots. So, are *you* emotionally ready to retire?

Question 2: Am I financially ready to retire?

"Do I have enough money to retire?" This is the big one and the first, not the second, question nearly everyone actually asks me. My usual answer is, "Yes, but maybe not with the income you'd prefer." Then we get to work on figuring it out in more detail.

To really answer this question, I find it's essential to create your own comprehensive retirement plan. The planning process includes developing a thorough understanding of the various factors unique to your specific financial situation and how those factors all relate to one another. Sounds complicated, but it's not really so hard when you break it all down.

To really answer this question, I find it's essential to create your own comprehensive retirement plan.

You're probably already asking most of the right questions to figure out if you're financially ready. Your questions are likely the same as those I've been hearing over and over from my clients all these years—and, most likely, the same questions I'll be answering in this book.

As you continue reading, the following chapters will cover specific questions to help you figure out if you're financially ready and, if so, to come up with a doable retirement plan for you. Broadly speaking, I've grouped these questions according to a few common themes:

- **How much money do I need?** Or, as I prefer to ask, what's your retirement spending plan? A spending plan is a crucial component of any retirement plan. It includes your expected monthly expenses for essentials such as housing, food, healthcare, and utilities as well as discretionary expenses such as travel, entertainment, and hobbies. I recommend making both a "basic" spending plan and a "dream" spending plan. Creating these plans will help you understand how much money you'll need to retire comfortably. You'll also have to plan for how long you need it to last—that is, how long you expect to live (chapter 2).

- **What are my retirement income sources?** Now that you know how much money you'll need during retirement, it's time to look at the income you'll have coming in to see if it will cover your expenses. If not, will you need to keep working, perhaps just part-time? Or can you cut back on your expenses and make ends meet?

  Calculating your income will involve answering more specific questions, such as "How much will your Social Security benefit be?" (chapter 3), "Which sort of pension income will you receive, if any?" (chapter 4), "When will you take distributions from your retirement accounts?" (chapter 5), and "How much income can you earn from other sources, such as after-tax investments, real estate, or even a part-time job?" (chapter 6)
- **How should I manage my retirement investments?** To maintain your desired lifestyle in retirement, it's essential to manage your investments wisely. Just as with your spending, this involves developing and following a strategy that's tailored to your situation. A good strategy also includes preparing to weather the financial storms you'll inevitably face—not the least of which is inflation—so that your retirement savings will last throughout your golden years (chapter 7).
- **What taxes will I pay during retirement?** The government won't stop taxing you just because you are no longer working. Retirement brings about new tax implications related to your new sources of retirement income. Understanding how taxes will impact your retirement income and coming up with tax strategies is crucial to a good retirement plan (chapter 8).

- **What financial threats will I face?** No matter how well you plan for retirement, you're sure to run into unexpected hazards—think catastrophic disease, a bad investment decision, or even falling prey to a financial scam—that threaten to derail your financial security. While nobody can plan for every possible calamity, there are plenty of steps you can take, beginning with educating yourself about the common threats facing retirees (chapter 9).
- **What sort of financial help is available?** While it's possible to plan for retirement and manage your finances on your own (including by reading books like this one), seeking the guidance of a financial planning professional can be invaluable. These experts will help you navigate the complexities—from understanding your income sources and creating a spending plan to managing investments and accounting for tax implications. Working with a professional will give you confidence and peace of mind (chapter 10).

Being financially ready requires careful planning. By understanding the various factors that impact retirement, such as your spending plan, income sources, investment strategy, taxation, and the unexpected, you can make an informed decision about when to retire and how to ensure your financial security throughout this time of life.

Being financially ready requires careful planning.

Chapter 2

How Much Money Do I Need?

Mike is an elderly doctor, still working, who believes he can't get by on less than $1 million a year. Even though he hired me as his financial advisor, Mike rarely sticks with my advice for long. His investments are always short-lived, since he ends up spending most of his money instead of leaving it invested. As a result, he has virtually nothing saved for retirement. When Mike asks me if he can afford to take a trip to Paris, I try to talk him out of it because I know where he's going to get the money: straight from what was supposed to be his retirement investments. If you ask Mike, he will tell you, with a straight face, that he doesn't live extravagantly but he does like his "toys"—nice cars, music equipment, even a private plane. He often says to me, "I just don't know how the 'average person' gets by."

Then there's my client Wilma, a widowed homemaker. She has a nice retirement nest egg and a good investment income, but she spends only a small percentage of it. She takes out just $16,000 a year from her retirement savings but still often asks me, "What am I going to do with all that leftover income at the end of the month?" Once, when I encouraged her to travel, she responded, "Where would I go?" I finally suggested she start with somewhere close to home: "How about a trip to Tulsa to visit the sewing machine museum?" (Tulsa is only about two hours away for her, and she likes to sew.) She loved the idea but wondered, "Can I really afford to do that?" "With your spending habits, yes, easily," I replied. I was so happy when she decided to take a trip to the museum. She couldn't stop telling me about it.

So how much do you need?

Question 3: What percentage of my pre-retirement income do I need during retirement?

This question comes up often. Most people have heard the general rule that you can maintain the same standard of living during retirement with 60% to 80% of your pre-retirement income. But where did this number come from, and why isn't it 100%?

It's because in retirement, your expenses will probably be less than in your working years. Why? You'll no longer need to sock away 15% of your income to fund a 401(k) or contribute to an individual retirement account (IRA) or otherwise save for retirement. You will also no longer be paying 7.65% of your earned income in FICA taxes (or 15.3% if you're self-employed). Then there are all the job-related expenses you won't be incurring: professional clothes, commuting costs, etc. That's why most people can live on less income during retirement.

> So you can't be so sure that the 60% to 80% rule will work for you.

But, as a general rule, general rules can be dangerous. What about increased healthcare costs as you age? How about all the travel adventures you've been waiting to take? Those new retirement expenses can really add up, so you can't be so sure that the 60% to 80% rule will work for you.

Instead of applying a general rule like that, I recommend you create your own budget—or as I prefer to call it, your *spending plan,* since most of us seem to prefer spending over budgeting. How much money should you plan to spend to live your unique retirement lifestyle? That's the next question …

Question 4: How can I plan my retirement spending to enjoy retirement now and not run out of money later?

Like this question implies, we all want to enjoy our retirement while we can, but we don't want to spend so much that we risk going broke in our later years. It's a balance. So how much can you spend to comfortably enjoy the retirement you've been dreaming of?

To figure out how much you'll need, it's good to run some numbers and then get it all down in writing. Some planning now can save a lot of heartache later, like running out of money! As you put together your spending plan, think about your lifestyle, your health, and your choices around money. To get you started, I've listed below some common expense categories that most retirees face and included a worksheet to help you create your own spending plan.

Some planning now can save a lot of heartache later, like running out of money!

Housing

- Mortgage or rent. Hopefully, you've paid off your house by the time you retire—or you're close to it. That's because if you haven't paid off your mortgage, those monthly payments will be a significant expense. If you have after-tax investments or excess cash, consider paying off your mortgage. But I *don't* recommend using retirement accounts to do this because of the often-heavy tax ramifications.

- Property taxes and insurance. Even if your mortgage is paid off, you'll still need to budget for these costs. While these are usually once-a-year payments, don't forget to include them in your monthly spending amount.
- Maintenance and repairs. You still have to keep up your home, including occasional major repairs. A rule of thumb for home annual repairs is 1% to 4% of the home's value, depending on factors such as the house's age, the cost of labor, and location.

Healthcare

- Health insurance. If you're not on Medicare yet, this can be a major expense. Check out Affordable Care Act coverage. And some associations, such as your local chamber of commerce, may offer other plans worth considering.
- Medicare premiums. While Medicare covers some healthcare costs, it's not free. Premiums for Part B in particular can be hefty. Know the cost and plan for it (see also the resources section at the end of this book).
- Supplemental health insurance. It's pretty important to buy a Medigap policy to cover what Medicare doesn't.
- Out-of-pocket costs. These include deductibles, copays, prescriptions, and other medical expenses, such as dental and vision, not covered by some insurance policies.

- Long-term care. Costs for assisted living, nursing home care, or in-home care can be a biggie for some people. These costs may include premiums for long-term care insurance or setting aside money yourself each month for future expenses (that is, "self-insuring") so that you won't deplete your retirement nest egg if you end up needing long-term care.

Utilities and Home Services

- Basic utilities. Retirees still have to pay monthly bills for gas, electricity, water, sewer, trash services, and the like.
- Phone/internet/cable.
- Housekeeping and maintenance services, if you choose to use them.

Groceries/Dining/Household

- Regular expenses for daily meals and basic household items.
- Social outings or convenience meals.

Transportation

- Car payments (if you have a loan) or payments to your savings (if you don't have a loan) in order to purchase your next car.
- Vehicle maintenance and fuel.
- Auto insurancc.
- Public transit fares if that's how you get around.

Insurance

- Life insurance, if you still carry a policy. This is a tricky decision that depends on your health. If you're in bad health, it's probably best to keep the policy. And if you're in good health and the risk you were paying premiums for is gone, then it likely makes sense to cash it in.

Personal Expenses

- Clothing, personal care, grooming, and other day-to-day personal expenses.
- Hobbies, leisure, and recreational activities (for me, that includes all my pickleball gear and gym membership).

Travel and Entertainment

- Vacations, if you're like the many retirees ready to travel. Do it while you can, but don't overdo it. I haven't seen very many sustainable spending plans that include monthly trips to Europe.
- Movies, concerts, sports tickets, and similar activities, which can quickly add up to some hefty sums!

Gifts and Contributions

- Charitable giving.
- Gifts for family and friends on special occasions and holidays.

Debts

- Any outstanding debts, such as car loans, credit card balances, personal loans, or medical bills. I recommend paying these off, preferably using after-tax accounts (not retirement pre-tax accounts). By paying credit card debt that's racking up interest at 18%, you are, in essence, making 18%, after tax, guaranteed. That's pretty good, I'd say.

Emergency Fund

- Hopefully, you already have money saved for emergencies or unexpected costs. A common recommendation is to have three to six months of monthly expenses invested somewhere safe and liquid so you can get to it quickly. You also need to plan to replenish this fund whenever you incur any emergency expenses (see also questions 43 and 44).

Remember, these are general categories, and your specific expenses will depend on your personal choices and circumstances. To create your own spending plan, write down all your expenses. Look over your first draft. Is this reasonable? Go back over it until it is. This plan won't be set in stone, but it needs to be a good ballpark estimate. Make sure to pause and feel good about your hard work. Then compare your planned spending to your retirement income. (The next question will help you figure out your income.) Hopefully, your income exceeds your expenses. If not, it's time to make some more adjustments. And if so, then you've completed your basic plan. Congratulations!

> **Why not plan for a few extras that you can enjoy now, if your finances allow?**

As a next step, I encourage you to create a "dream" spending plan—one that goes beyond your basic plan but still falls within your retirement income amount. Why not plan for a few extras that you can enjoy now, if your finances allow?

Lastly, be sure to revisit your spending plan from time to time. It's always wise to make adjustments based on rising costs due to inflation, especially for big-ticket categories such as healthcare and housing. Then there's the fact that your spending is likely to change as you grow older, particularly since your retirement years may measure in the decades. Adapting your plan over time is crucial for a comfortable and secure retirement.

SPENDING PLAN WORKSHEET		
Expense	**Monthly amount**	**Yearly total**
Housing:		
Mortgage/rent		
Taxes/insurance		
Maintenance/repairs		
Healthcare:		
Health insurance/Medicare premiums		
Supplemental health insurance		
Dental/vision		
Out-of-pocket costs		
Long-term care		
Utilities/home services:		
Basic utilities (gas, electricity, water, etc.)		
Phone/internet cable		
Housekeeping/maintenance services		
Groceries/dining/household:		
Daily meals and household items		
Social outings or convenience meals		
Transportation:		
Car payments (or savings for a new car)		
Vehicle maintenance and fuel		
Auto insurance		
Public transit fares		
Life insurance		
Clothing, personal care, grooming, etc.		
Hobbies/leisure/recreational activities		
Travel/vacations		
Entertainment (movies, concerts, etc.)		
Charitable giving		
Gifts/special occasions		
Debts (personal loan, credit card balance, medical bills)		
Emergency fund savings		
Miscellaneous		
BASIC RETIREMENT SPENDING TOTAL		
Dream retirement extras (epic vacation, home remodeling, etc.)		
DREAM RETIREMENT SPENDING TOTAL		

Question 5: Once I no longer have a paycheck (which is kind of scary!), where will my retirement income come from?

Most people's retirement income comes from a few primary sources. Each source has different characteristics—pros and cons. The amount you'll receive from each income source will also differ according to your situation. Below, I describe the main sources of most people's retirement income. Then, in the following chapters, we'll dig deeper into each type, deeper meaning the various choices you have, tax considerations, the best time to tap into each source, etc.

- **Social Security.** The first income source available to almost all retirees is Social Security (see also chapter 3). It's essentially a government-run pension plan funded by contributions made by individuals who worked hard over the years. This savings program was designed back in the 1930s as a safety net to support the elderly, widows, and fatherless children. For many, Social Security remains the backbone of retirement income, providing a steady stream of cash that's adjusted annually for inflation. How and when you begin to collect your Social Security benefit is, well, another question. And don't forget that Social Security was never meant to shoulder the entire burden. In fact, it's really tough to live on Social Security alone. So, hopefully, you'll also have some of the following income sources.

  Don't forget that Social Security was never meant to shoulder the entire burden.

- **Pension plans.** The good old-fashioned company- or government-sponsored pension plan (or *defined-benefit plan* as we financial planner types call it) can be another comforting, steady stream of income in your retirement years (see also chapter 4). Pensions begin paying a defined benefit at a certain age based on varying factors. Generally, it's a monthly benefit, often tied to inflation, that you'll receive for the rest of your life. Sadly, pensions are becoming the financial world's dodo bird, an endangered species, as companies shift much of the responsibility of retirement savings onto employees. If you're among the fortunate few with a defined-benefit plan, treasure it!

Pensions are becoming the financial world's dodo bird, an endangered species.

- **Defined-contribution retirement accounts.** The everyman alternatives to a pension include the wonderful 401(k) retirement plan and its nonprofit/governmental cousins, the 403(b) and 457, which are what we call *defined-contribution plans.* With these tax-advantaged savings plans, you make a defined contribution while you're working, often matched by your employer, with either pre-tax dollars ("traditional" option) or after-tax dollars whose earnings will be tax-free later ("Roth" option). Matching contributions, a tax deduction, tax-deferred growth—that's why I call these options wonderful. They have become a significant part of Americans' retirement savings, as they are a great wealth-accumulation tool with tax-saving benefits (see also chapter 5).
- **Individual retirement accounts (IRAs).** IRAs are another big source of income for many retirees (see also chapter 5). An IRA is also a tax-advantaged retirement savings account, but you decide for yourself how much of your earnings to

contribute to your IRA (up to certain dollar limitations). That's different from contributions to 401(k)s and the like, which are made through automatic deductions from your paycheck. IRAs come in the same two flavors as the plans described above—traditional and Roth. Traditional IRAs offer tax deductions now, with taxes paid upon withdrawal, whereas Roth IRAs allow you to contribute after-tax dollars, with the enticing promise of tax-free withdrawals during retirement. Both types are great options.

- **Other income sources.** Don't ignore other potential sources of retirement income, such as an after-tax securities account, real estate rentals, personal savings, and even part-time employment. There's also the option of a reverse mortgage, which allows homeowners to convert a portion of their home equity into income. Finally, there are those who may receive a windfall from an inheritance or the sale of a business. These can all contribute significantly to your financial security in retirement (see also chapter 6).

Hopefully, you'll have diverse sources of retirement income. By combining these income streams—and applying the tax strategies you'll read about later—you'll be much more likely to weather financial storms and enjoy a comfortable income for life. In the end, it's all about creating the retirement that you envision for yourself and having the income to live it.

Hopefully, you'll have diverse sources of retirement income.

RETIREMENT INCOME WORKSHEET		
Source	**Monthly amount**	**Yearly total**
Social Security benefit		
Pension		
Defined-contribution retirement accounts (401(k), 403(b), 457 plans)		
IRAs (traditional and Roth)		
After-tax investments and savings accounts		
Real estate rental income		
Part-time employment income		
Reverse mortgage payments		
Other income		
TOTAL		

Question 6: How long do I need my money to last?

The short answer is, your money should last as long as *you* last. Some retirees will say they also want to leave money for their children, and that's great. But to me, the best thing you can do for your kids is first to make sure you take care of *you*.

At first blush, "as long as you last" can be understood as life expectancy. Life expectancy is the number of additional years, from now, that you have a fifty-fifty chance of living. You can find lots of life expectancy tables that estimate that number. The table below shows the Social Security Administration's estimated life expectancy for 2025, broken down by age and gender. (This chart is updated every year, so be sure to take a look for the latest data.)

LIFE EXPECTANCY		
At age	**Male life expectancy** (in remaining years)	**Female life expectancy** (in remaining years)
60	20.41	23.65
65	16.95	19.75
70	13.69	16.0
75	10.62	12.49
80	7.92	9.38
85	5.65	6.72
Source: Social Security Actuarial Life Table https://www.ssa.gov/oact/STATS/table4c6.html		

So, for example, if you were a 65-year-old male in 2025, you had a fifty-fifty chance of making it another 16.95 years—or just shy of your 82nd birthday.

Sadly, Americans' life expectancy has actually gotten shorter in recent years. The numbers also vary according to other factors such as race, ethnicity, socioeconomic status, and even geographical location.

There are many other factors that better predict your particular life expectancy.

But there are many other factors that better predict your particular life expectancy, such as the following:

- Current health
- Diet
- Tobacco use
- Alcohol consumption
- Exercise

- Genetics (a tough one to control)
- Body composition

I've found some great online life expectancy calculators that take these (and other) factors into consideration. These are some of my favorites:

- Life Expectancy Calculator.[2] Answer about 20 short questions and get immediate results by email.
- Healthy Life Expectancy Calculator.[3] Another short questionnaire. I like this one because it predicts the longest life for me!
- Living to 100 Life Expectancy Calculator.[4] This longer questionnaire also generates suggestions for adding years to your life.

I'm writing this book at age 66, and running through some of these calculators, I have a life expectancy of another 27 to 30 years.

But planning for your retirement based on your life expectancy has a built-in problem. Since life expectancy is an average, there's a 50% chance you'll live longer and run out of money before you run out of life. A plan with a 50% chance of failure doesn't sound like a good plan to me.

Planning for your retirement based on your life expectancy has a built-in problem.

A better plan is to figure on living to age 100—unless there's a good reason to believe you won't. Think that is a little long? Don't be so sure. The probability may be higher than you think. For myself, I

2 https://lifeexpectancycalculator.com/

3 https://apps.goldensoncenter.uconn.edu/HLEC/

4 https://www.livingto100.com/

used an online calculator to determine that my probability of reaching 100 is 8%. Visit the Actuaries Longevity Illustrator[5] to learn more about longevity versus life expectancy.

I recommend, in most cases, planning to age 100.

Now, you might be thinking, I don't know if I really *want* to live that long. But if you do make it to such a ripe old age, you'll want your money to last that long, no? So, I recommend, in most cases, planning to age 100.

Question 7: How should I plan so that my retirement income will keep pace with inflation?

"Inflation is when you pay $15 for the $10 haircut you used to get for $5 when you had hair."
—**Sam Ewing**

I consider the inevitable increase in the cost of living (otherwise known as *inflation*) to be the biggest risk that many retirees fail to plan for.

The inevitable increase in the cost of living (otherwise known as *inflation*) is the biggest risk that many retirees fail to plan for.

So, this is a critical question, since many of us will rely on our retirement income for 30 years or more. Here are some common strategies people might follow in order to deal with inflation. I'll start with the ugly and end with the best.

5 https://www.longevityillustrator.org/

1. "I'll plan to live on a fixed retirement income and then reduce my spending each year to compensate for increases in the cost of living."

The cost of living has decreased only once since 1960, so planning to live on a fixed income that doesn't include future increases is what I'll call the "ugly" plan. For those who remember the 1980s (and that probably includes you), inflation hit over 14%! At that rate, the cost of living doubles about every five years, so over a period of 10 years, your purchasing power would be reduced to just one-fourth of where it started. Who can adjust their spending to account for that large a decrease in spending power? Hopefully, we'll never see that level of inflation again, but I would have a better plan than this just in case we do.

2. "Historically, inflation averages about 3% a year, so I'll plan on increasing my retirement income by 3% each year."

This strategy is "better," but it's not good enough. Planning to increase one's retirement income by a constant 3% a year reminds me of the parable about the guy who's not worried about wading across a river because its average depth is only one foot. He drowned. Taking into account the historical average is not necessarily bad for planning purposes, but you need to build in additional protection, since inflation will be higher than that from time to time.

Taking into account the historical average is not necessarily bad for planning purposes, but you need to build in additional protection.

3. "I'll increase my retirement income each year based on the Consumer Price Index (CPI)."

I consider this strategy "better still," since it adjusts annually and is based on a "real-life" percentage. But the problem with the CPI is that it doesn't take into account a retiree's "basket of goods" (commonly purchased goods and services); it looks at the cost of goods for consumers of all ages.

4. "I'll increase my retirement income each year based on the CPI for Americans aged 62 or older (R-CPI-E)."

For the "best" strategy, I recommend planning based on the R-CPI-E, which specifically accounts for the basket of goods most closely resembling the actual spending patterns of people 62 years and older. (You can learn more on the R-CPI-E home page.[6])

> For the "best" strategy, I recommend planning based on the R-CPI-E.

To generate an income that adapts successfully to cost-of-living increases, you'll need an investment plan that is flexible and has inflation hedges, that is, investments that go up in value with inflation. More on this in future questions ...

* * *

In this chapter, we've covered a lot of ground in figuring out how much money you'll actually need in retirement, and I hope you'll agree: It's probably not as difficult as you thought. We've debunked the one-size-fits-all 60% to 80% of pre-retirement income

---

6 https://www.bls.gov/cpi/research-series/r-cpi-e-home.htm

rule (because your retirement needs are as unique as you are), walked through creating your own spending plan, and mapped out where your retirement income will actually come from. We've also tackled the big question of how long your money needs to last (because running out of money at age 95 is not the plot twist anyone wants in their retirement story) and reviewed strategies to secure your savings against that sneaky thief inflation.

Next, we'll take a deeper dive into Social Security, since this government-run safety net will likely be one of your key income sources. As you'll see, the rules around Social Security can be as complex as they are important—and making the wrong decision can cost you thousands of dollars a month. Let's make sure that doesn't happen to you.

Chapter 3

Social Security Income

"Guess what?" my client Susan asked. She was bouncing up and down in her chair, giddy. I'd never seen her this happy. Now 59 years and 10 months of age, Susan had been my client for over twenty years. She had been through a lot recently, having lost her husband to cancer only a year earlier. Being by his side through it all had taken a toll on her, so to see her so happy today was a wonderful change.

"I give up," I said. "What?"

Her eyes sparkled as she stuck out her left hand. On her ring finger sat a large diamond solitaire. She told me she had been seeing someone lately and didn't think it would work out at first, but …

"You're engaged?" I blurted out. I was *so* hoping for this answer.

"No, silly, I'm married!"

I noticed myself forcing a smile as I replied, "Congratulations. I'm happy for you." I really was happy for her, but my financial planner heart sank. Had Susan waited just a few more months before remarrying, she would have been eligible for Social Security surviving spouse benefits, which in her case would have put about $2,700 more in her pocket each month. Given her financial situation, she most certainly could use it. But by marrying when she did, at age 59, she no longer met two important requirements for this benefit—being age 60 or older and being an unmarried, surviving spouse. Now she could not apply for these funds.

Susan learned the hard way how important it can be to understand the ins and outs of Social Security benefits, and she missed out on a great source of retirement income.

Question 8: Where do I find my Social Security benefit information, and what does it show?

The Social Security Administration website (ssa.gov)[7] has an almost scary amount of information for and about you. To access your personal information, you first have to create an account at login.gov or ID.me and then set up your "My Social Security" account. Once you've done so, you can see your "full earnings record" since you began working, probably many decades ago. It may feel a little odd to know that the government has been tracking what you've been earning for so many years, including that part-time, minimum-wage job you had when you were 16 years old. But it's good they have, since the amount of your future benefits is based on all those earnings (or, more precisely, your 35 highest-earning years).

One feature I really love on the Social Security website is the Plan for Retirement[8] estimator that calculates the monthly payment you will receive according to when you decide to retire and begin collecting benefits. It automatically lists your estimated monthly minimum

7 https://www.ssa.gov/

8 https://www.ssa.gov/retirement/plan-for-retirement

benefit if you retire “early” (age 62), full benefit if you retire at your “full” retirement age (FRA) (age 67 for those born in 1960 and later), and maximum benefit if you “delay” your retirement to age 70 (the age when your monthly benefit amount tops out). You can also enter a different retirement age than those three to see the effect on your benefit amount. And if you are still working, you can change the amount of your average future annual salary to see how that will affect your benefit. Remember, these are just estimates based on your current earnings record. If you have an additional year of income or if the laws governing Social Security change, your benefit amounts will change, too.

The Social Security website will also show you the following details:

- Your full retirement age based on your birthday
- The amount you can earn before being penalized if you start taking benefits early
- How paying for Medicare Part B can impact the amount you receive
- An estimate of what your spouse or children might receive in survivor benefits if you die
- If, heaven forbid, you become disabled and can’t work, an estimate of your monthly disability benefit
- Details on whether you have earned enough credits to qualify for Medicare at age 65
- Answers to almost any other question you might have in a great frequently asked questions section

If going online isn't your thing, you can also request a paper statement be mailed to you, or you can visit a local Social Security office. However, the online option tends to be the most convenient for most people.

A word about security: Always make sure you're on the official ssa.gov website before inputting any personal information. Look for "https://" at the beginning of the web address, which indicates you're on a secure site. You can also verify any website's security certificate if you're unsure; in most browsers, it's as simple as clicking on the little padlock icon to the left of the website in the address bar.

Always make sure you're on the official ssa.gov website before inputting any personal information.

Question 9: How is my Social Security benefit amount calculated?

This question often comes with many other twists. For example, "If I delay taking Social Security and make zero dollars in those years, will my benefit amount be less?" or "If I delay retirement a year or two but take a part-time job, how will my benefit amount be affected?"

To answer these sorts of questions, it's helpful to understand how your benefits are calculated. That calculation begins with your earnings record. An easy way to find your Social Security earnings is to visit the Social Security Administration website (see question 8). Just log in to (or set up) your account and then open your Social Security statement to review

An easy way to find your Social Security earnings is to visit the Social Security Administration website.

your entire earnings history. (While you're there, be sure to appreciate how far you've come!) Now, armed with your earnings history, here's how your benefit amount is calculated.

First, Social Security takes all your earning years since birth and adjusts (or indexes) your earnings based on the national average wage index. This isn't quite the same as the cost-of-living adjustment (COLA) amount, but the concept is the same. Indexing is designed to account for inflation and equalize the value of income from 40 years ago, when a dime really was worth a dime, as compared to today, when "a nickel ain't worth a dime anymore," as the baseball sage Yogi Berra famously complained.

Next, they take your 35 highest adjusted earning years. (Why 35? There's probably a good reason, but I'm not sure what it is.) If you didn't work for 35 years, then zero dollars are entered for the years you didn't earn anything. Anytime you work and pay into Social Security, whether it's a part-time or full-time job, your benefits will increase if that year is among your top 35 adjusted earning years. That's true even after you've begun collecting benefits. Then, your top 35 years of indexed earnings are added up and divided by the total number of months to calculate the average. The fancy term for this is *average indexed monthly earnings* (AIME).

To complicate things a bit, there's also a cap to the amount of earnings that can be counted for any year. Anything you make over the cap doesn't count toward your retirement benefits. The table below shows the maximum earnings cap in recent years:

MAXIMUM TAXABLE EARNINGS EACH YEAR THAT COUNT TOWARD SOCIAL SECURITY RETIREMENT	
Year	**Amount**
2016	$118,500
2017	$127,200
2018	$128,400
2019	$132,900
2020	$137,700
2021	$142,800
2022	$147,000
2023	$160,200
2024	$168,600
2025	$176,100
Source: Social Security Maximum Taxable Earnings https://www.ssa.gov/benefits/retirement/planner/ageincrease.html	

Are you still with me? Great. Now, bend points are used to calculate what's called your primary insurance amount (PIA). *Bend point* is another fancy term that refers to the fact that different income amounts are weighted differently. For you analytical types, here's how the PIA was calculated for 2025[9]:

- 90% of the first $1,226 of AIME
- Plus 32% of any amount over $1,226 up to $7,391
- Plus 15% of any amount over $7,391

You can see that PIA is heavily weighted to the first portion of

9 "Primary Insurance Amount," Social Security Administration, accessed September 9, 2025, https://www.ssa.gov/oact/COLA/piaformula.html. Be sure to check the SSA website for the most up-to-date amounts.

income. This weighting helps low-wage earners, who will depend on Social Security income the most.

Finally, your PIA is the monthly amount you will receive if you begin collecting Social Security benefits at your full retirement age (FRA). If you begin collecting sooner than your FRA, your benefit will be less. And if you wait to begin collecting until after your FRA, your benefit will be more (see also question 10).

And that's it. Calculating your benefit amount may feel a bit convoluted, but armed with this knowledge, you will make better financial decisions as you approach retirement. For example, if you're not taking Social Security benefits yet, you shouldn't worry about that part-time job negatively impacting your Social Security calculation (aka, the earned income rule). It can only help you. It's kind of like heads you win, tails you break even. (More on this in question 10 as well.)

Question 10: What do I need to know about my full retirement age?

Full retirement age (FRA) is the age at which you qualify to receive your full Social Security retirement benefit amount. FRA is different for different people, based on the year they were born. I could explain the math formula the government uses to calculate your FRA, but it's much easier if I show you the different FRAs in the following table:

SOCIAL SECURITY FRA	
If you were born in:	**Your FRA is:**
1943–1954	66 years
1955	66 years, 2 months
1956	66 years, 4 months
1957	66 years, 6 months
1958	66 years, 8 months
1959	66 years, 10 months
1960 and later	67 years
Source: Social Security Maximum Taxable Earnings	

There are two important factors to understand once you know your FRA.

First, the amount of your monthly benefit will be either reduced or increased depending on whether you start collecting Social Security *before* or *after* your FRA. Even if you're eligible to start your benefits at 62, doing so will come at a steep reduction to your monthly benefit amount—generally a permanent reduction—compared to your monthly benefit if you wait until reaching your FRA (see question 11 for the details). On the other hand, if you wait to start receiving Social Security benefits until after you hit your FRA, your monthly benefit amount will be increased according to the number of months you wait past your FRA, up to age 70 (see question 12 for the details). This works out to be about an 8% bump for each year you wait. But at age 70, your increase is capped, so there's zero benefit to beginning collecting any time after the month you turn 70.

The second important factor to understand is the *earned income rule* that's applied before you reach your FRA. If you choose to take Social Security retirement benefits before reaching your FRA and you also continue to earn any income, you can only make so much earned income before they hammer you by holding back a big chunk of your benefits. (Technically, they give it back to you starting once you reach your FRA, but it will be amortized over your life expectancy. This sure won't feel like a good trade-off when you see that reduction in your check now.)

To elaborate, if you start collecting Social Security at age 62, you can make up to $23,400 in earned income (that was the 2025 annual limit) without affecting your benefits. But for every $2 you make over that limit, Uncle Sam will deduct $1 from your benefit payment. Brutal. If you wait to start collecting benefits until anytime in the same calendar year as your FRA but before you reach your actual FRA month, it won't be nearly as bad. For every $3 you make over the limit ($62,160 for 2025), Uncle Sam will deduct $1 in benefits.[10]

Here are two examples I adapted from the Social Security website:

- Say you are two years under your FRA and entitled to receive $800 a month in benefits (or $9,600 for the entire year). If you earn $33,400 (which is $10,000 over the $23,400 limit for 2025), then your Social Security benefits would be reduced by $5,000 ($1 for every $2 you earned over the limit). That means you would receive $4,600 of your $9,600 in benefits for the year ($9,600 – $5,000 = $4,600).
- Say you will reach your FRA in the month of August and work the seven previous months (January through July) before you retire. And assume you are entitled to $800 per month in benefits (or $9,600 for the year). If you earn $65,160 (which

10 "Special Earnings Limit Rule," Social Security Administration, accessed September 9, 2025, https://www.ssa.gov/benefits/retirement/planner/rule.html. Be sure to check the SSA website for the most up-to-date amounts.

is $3,000 over the $62,160 limit for 2025 in the seven months before your FRA), then your Social Security benefits will be reduced by $1,000 ($1 for every $3 you earned over the limit). That means you will receive $4,600 of your $5,600 benefits for the first seven months ($5,600 – $1,000 = $4,600). Beginning in August, when you reach your FRA, you will receive your full benefit ($800 per month), no matter how much you earn. Seems it's better to have a late-in-the-year birthday. You did plan for that before being born, didn't you?

Once you finally hit your FRA, the earned income rule goes away. You'll face no penalty regardless of your earned income. Keep in mind, I'm talking about earned income here, which means wages and any net profit from self-employment income. Other income—from pensions, annuities, interest, investments, veterans' benefits, or rental properties (in most cases)—isn't subject to those limits. Yes, I know this doesn't make a lot of sense, but as I often say, tax laws don't have to make sense and don't have to be fair. Understand them (or find someone who does) and strategize accordingly.

As you can see, knowing your FRA can help you decide when to begin collecting your Social Security benefit. You can calculate the reduction for beginning earlier or the increase for beginning later. And you can avoid the earned income land mine. In essence, grasping the concept of FRA is one of the keys to locking in an optimal Social Security income for life. After the marathon of your career—and paying into Social Security for all those years—this is one victory you richly deserve.

Grasping the concept of FRA is one of the keys to locking in an optimal Social Security income for life.

Question 11: Should I begin collecting my Social Security benefit before I reach my full retirement age?

Getting those benefits early sounds appealing, doesn't it? But like most things, it comes at a cost. If you're thinking about collecting Social Security before your full retirement age (FRA), here are some factors for you to consider.

Collecting earlier will cost you a *reduction in your monthly benefit amount*—and the earlier you start taking Social Security, the bigger the reduction. To make matters worse, this reduction in your benefit will continue for the rest of your life. Your benefit amount won't go back up once you hit your FRA. (There's one exception to this described below.)

Getting those benefits early sounds appealing, doesn't it? But like most things, it comes at a cost.

Your reduction for collecting early is calculated based on the number of months between when you begin your benefits and your FRA (see questions 9 and 10 regarding calculating your benefits and FRA). If you begin collecting less than 36 months before FRA, your monthly benefit will be reduced by 5/9 of 1% for each month you claim early. And if you begin more than 36 months before FRA, your monthly benefit is reduced by an additional 5/12 of 1% for each month beyond those first 36 months.[11]

For example, if you begin collecting at 62 and your FRA is 67, that's a total of 60 months early. Doing the math, that means 24 months times 5/12 of 1% (or 10%) plus 36 months times 5/9 of 1% (or 20%), which adds up to a 30% reduction in your monthly benefit

11 "Benefit Reduction for Early or Late Retirement," Social Security Administration, accessed September 9, 2025, https://www.ssa.gov/oact/quickcalc/earlyretire.html.

amount. That's a pretty big hit. Or say you wait to retire until you hit 65; your benefits will still be reduced by about 13.3%.

The government does give you up to 12 months to change your mind if you start taking benefits early. (That's the exception I mentioned above.) If you decide to stop your early benefits within the first 12 months, you can repay whatever you've already collected and pretend it never happened. But you can only do this one time.

Next, by collecting early, you risk stepping on the *earned income reduction* land mine. In a nutshell, if you begin taking benefits before reaching your FRA *and* you keep working, you will be penalized for every dollar you earn above a certain amount (see also question 10 for more on how big a hit you might take). Fortunately, once you reach your FRA, you can earn any amount without penalties or limits. That's right: If you're past your retirement age, you're allowed to keep working without reducing your benefit amount, but not before. Yes, sounds crazy, but those are the Social Security rules.

By collecting early, you risk stepping on the earned income reduction land mine.

So, armed with all this information, should you begin collecting Social Security benefits before you reach your FRA? Here's the general decision tree I use:

1. Do you expect to keep working and make more than the earned income limit, even by a slight amount? If your answer is yes, then my general rule is: No, don't take your benefit early.
2. If you plan to stop working (and are fairly certain you're not going to exceed the earned income limit), then … Do you need your benefits now? If your answer is yes, then my general rule is: Yes, take your benefit early.

3. If you don't need the money, then my general rule depends on your life expectancy. Do you think you have a 50% chance of living past the age of 82? (Yes, I know that's a tough question to answer with any certainty.) If your answer is, "No way I'll live past 82," then my general rule is: Yes, take your benefit early (most likely at your FRA or maybe earlier if you're not working). But if your answer is, "There's a pretty good chance I'll make it past 82," then my general rule is: Wait until age 70 to collect your benefit.

If your answer is, "There's a pretty good chance I'll make it past 82," then my general rule is: Wait until age 70 to collect your benefit.

Of course, that's just my own general thought process, and you may have other factors and situations to consider. Plus, a decision like this isn't just about the numbers. Perhaps you want to take that big vacation and see the world "while you still can," and the only way to make it happen is with your monthly Social Security benefit income. Or maybe you have personal issues, health issues, or a job loss, to name a few other considerations. Each of us brings our unique circumstances into our decision on whether to collect Social Security early.

There are also some specific situations that can alter your numbers and affect your decision, such as the following:

- You are a surviving spouse and are past the age of 60. (Remember Susan's story?)
- Your spouse has a much higher income record than you do.
- You're divorced but were married longer than 10 years.

All of these situations trigger specific decision tree rules and require a separate analysis and considerations beyond what I can explain here. In fact, this is a great example of why I recommend you consult a certified public accountant (CPA) or Certified Financial Planner® (CFP®) who specializes in retirement issues to help you sort out some of the complicated details. I wish Susan had done that—and I bet she does, too.

Question 12: Should I begin to take benefits when I reach full retirement age, or should I wait until I reach age 70?

This is an easier question to answer than the previous one about taking benefits before reaching full retirement age (FRA). That's because you no longer have to worry about the earned income test once you hit your FRA. You can make as much as you want without those earnings decreasing your benefits.

For every year you wait past your FRA, up to age 70, you'll typically see an increase of 8% in your benefit amount. Nice!

Here are the *benefits* of delaying Social Security past your FRA:

- **Increased monthly benefit amount.** For every year you wait past your FRA, up to age 70, you'll typically see an increase of 8% in your benefit amount. Nice!
- **Larger survivor benefits.** If you're married, your survivor's benefits grow past your FRA. It's hard to get prematurely motivated to use it, but if your benefit at death is larger than your spouse's benefit, then their total benefit will be increased to what yours would have been.

- **Delay paying income taxes on your Social Security.** Up to 85% of your Social Security may be included in your taxable income, depending on your situation. By delaying collecting Social Security benefits and instead drawing down other retirement assets (for example, after-tax accounts), you can reduce the amount of income that's subject to taxation and simultaneously allow your future Social Security benefit amount to increase. A good combo. When it comes to taxes, as the Bible says, "Render unto Caesar what is Caesar's," and as I like to add, "But not any more than that" (see also question 37 in the chapter on tax strategies).

The *disadvantage* of delaying Social Security is missing out on monthly checks.

Here's the decision tree I generally use when making the decision to delay after your FRA and up until age 70:

1. Do you need the money? If so, then my general rule is: Take it now.
2. If you don't need the money, then my general rule depends on your life expectancy. Do you think you have a 50% chance of living past the age of 82? (Still a tough question.) If your answer is, "No way I'll live past 82," then my general rule says: Take it now.

Do you need the money? If so, then my general rule is: Take it now.

3. But if your answer is, "Yes, there's a pretty good chance I'll make it past 82," then my general rule says: Wait until age 70 to collect your benefit.

As with the decision to collect benefits early, this is my *general* analytical calculation. But there are other factors specific to you, such as that big vacation or family issues. Be sure to consider your individual situation beyond the generic calculation.

Question 13: Will my Social Security benefit keep up with inflation?

In theory, yes. In reality, no.

Let's start with the theory. Social Security benefit amounts include a cost-of-living adjustment (COLA) each year. The annual COLA is based on the CPI-W (CPI for Urban Wage Earners and Clerical Workers). This adjustment is designed so that your Social Security benefit will keep pace with the rising cost of simply living and breathing on this earth—that is, inflation.

Then there's the reality. Some critics (including me) argue that the CPI-W doesn't accurately reflect the rate of inflation actually experienced by retirees. Their basket of goods (commonly purchased goods and services) is not the same as what's included in the CPI-W and generally rises more than the CPI-W, especially given the relatively high healthcare costs many older individuals face. In fact, according to The Senior Citizens League's research, Social Security benefits in 2024 were worth only about 80 cents on the dollar compared to 2010, in large part due to inadequate COLAs.[12]

To make things worse, Congress has been looking at changing the COLA so that it will be based on what's called the *chained CPI*. (For you analytical types, the difference is related to geometric averages versus arithmetic averages.) This is estimated to decrease COLA

12 "Loss of Buying Power 2024," The Senior Citizens League, July 16, 2024, https://seniorsleague.org/assets/TSCL-LOBP-Report-2024.pdf.

adjustments by 0.25% a year, which would lower annual increases to the benefit amount even more.

As it is, the COLA is also highly variable. It's been as low as zero in 2010, 2011, and 2016. Do you really think healthcare and food costs (pretty big line items for retirees) stayed the same in those years? On the high side, it's gone up as much as 14.3% in 1980. So, while it's nice that there are COLAs attached to Social Security benefits, the reality is they will probably not keep pace with the rate of inflation for a retiree's basket of goods.

> **The reality is that COLAs will probably not keep pace with the rate of inflation.**

Of course, there's not much you can do about your benefit amount—other than be aware, keep an eye on your expenses, and write your congressperson whenever Social Security changes are up for debate.

* * *

Social Security may seem straightforward—work for years, pay your taxes, then collect your benefits when you retire. But as Susan learned the hard way, timing can be everything. Whether you're navigating the maze of FRA, trying to decode the government's creative math behind benefit calculations (seriously, who came up with *bend points*?), or weighing the pros and cons of taking benefits early versus waiting until age 70, understanding Social Security rules can literally be worth tens of thousands of dollars over your lifetime.

The key takeaways: Know your FRA, understand how working affects your benefits if you claim early, and remember that every year you delay past your FRA until age 70 nets you about an 8% increase—a really nice bump even if you miss out on checks for a year or three.

But don't forget, even though Social Security's annual COLAs may be designed to help your benefits keep pace with inflation, the reality is that they often fall short of covering the actual rising costs that retirees face, especially healthcare expenses.

While Social Security may form the foundation of your retirement income, let's talk next about another potential cornerstone of your financial future—if you're fortunate enough to have this one—your pension plan.

Chapter 4

Pension Plans

Donna had been friends with my wife for many years, but she hadn't previously sought my advice—until now. Donna and her husband, Derek, were both on Social Security, and he had a nice pension. Their monthly income had been more than enough. Then she lost Derek to an aggressive cancer and needed help from a financial professional.

Donna was expecting that both of their Social Security checks would continue after her husband passed, but she was wrong. In reality, she was left with just one check, the higher of the two, and that's it. The real gut punch, though, was that the pension payments stopped entirely. Derek had selected the "single life only" option (that is, for *his* life) when setting up his pension payments. When he made that decision, he was in good health, and it was Donna who had some health issues. I'm sure his choice seemed like the smart one to him at the time. But since Derek ended up going first, all his pension income ended. Many tears were shed as we talked about Donna's remaining options, none of which were good. It was too late for me to help much.

The most important, and often irreversible, pension decision you'll make is which payout option to choose. So, it's critical to understand this issue—and others—about your pension. Answers to the following questions will help you do that.

The most important, and often irreversible, pension decision you'll make is which payout option to choose.

Question 14: What are all the payout options for my pension plan?

Congratulations. If you're asking this question, then you're probably one of those people fortunate enough to have a pension plan. As usual, there's no one-size-fits-all answer. Different pension plans have different payout options.

When you're about to retire, or just looking at your future options, you'll likely receive a notice describing your particular pension payout options. This may come from your employer's HR department or directly from the retirement plan. Below are some of the common options you may be choosing among:

1. **Lump sum distribution.** Some pension plans offer the option to take all or a portion of your pension benefits in a single lump sum payment rather than as a series of monthly payments over time. Taking a lump sum can provide a large amount of capital immediately, which you can invest as you see fit. But remember, you'll then be responsible for managing that money for the rest of your retirement.

2. **Annuity payments.** This is the traditional form of pension payout in which you receive a fixed monthly amount for the

rest of your life. No hassles and easy. Depending on your pension plan, you might have several annuity options to choose from:

- *Single life annuity.* This option provides a monthly benefit for the rest of your life. It will likely be the option that pays the highest monthly amount, since it only covers one life, yours. But beware: When you pass away, so does the monthly benefit. Your surviving spouse will no longer get anything. (This was the choice that Donna's husband, Derek, made, leaving her with no pension income after his death.)
- *Joint and survivor annuity.* With this option, you'll receive a monthly payment for the rest of your life, but it will be a lower amount than for a single life annuity. Then, upon your death, your designated beneficiary (usually a spouse) will continue to receive a monthly benefit, albeit typically just a percentage of your original benefit amount.
- *Period certain annuity.* This option will pay you a benefit for a certain period, for instance, 10 years. Once that period ends, even if you're still going strong, your benefit will end, and you won't receive anything more. But if you pass away before that period ends, your beneficiary will then receive your benefits until the period ends.
- *Other variations.* Some pension plans may offer combinations of the above options. For example, "life with 10 years certain" would pay benefits for life or 10 years, whichever is longer.

3. **Partial lump sum with reduced monthly annuity payments.** Some plans offer a combination option in which you can take a portion of your pension as a lump sum when you retire and then receive reduced monthly annuity payments.

4. **Early or deferred retirement.** Whether you opt for a lump sum or annuity, you might have the option to start receiving pension benefits immediately, even if you take an early retirement (that is, *before* the plan's stated retirement age) or to delay receiving benefits if you take a deferred retirement (that is, *after* the plan's stated retirement age). If you retire early, you'll receive a lower payout per month. If you defer retirement, you'll get more.

5. **Pension payments from a previous employer.** If you think you might be vested in a pension plan from a previous employer, you will probably qualify to receive a reduced benefit. Even if you held that job a long time ago, it's worth checking. I had a client who discovered he had a $1,400-a-month lifetime pension benefit from a previous job—some very good news indeed!

6. **Pension buybacks or purchases.** If you had periods when you weren't contributing to your pension, you might have the opportunity to "buy back" or "purchase" these years to increase your pension benefit. Maybe you had a period of unpaid leave, or you began working for your employer before they instituted the pension plan. I've also seen this with teachers who worked in different states. For instance, someone who first taught in Oklahoma and then finished their teaching career in Texas may be able to "buy years." This is generally a great deal if you can come up with the

cash to do so. That's because the return on buying back those years, when you do the calculation, is typically very high. But finding out if this is an option for you—and how to do it—is generally a challenge. It's best to ask your HR department if your pension plan offers any "buying years back" options.

These are the most common choices people have to make about their pensions when retiring. Now you're probably wondering how to evaluate your options and decide what's right for you. Read on.

Question 15: How should I choose between a lump sum and annuity?

Choosing between taking a lump sum payout and receiving a monthly annuity benefit is often the first big decision anyone has to make when it comes time to begin collecting on a pension. (Of course, the assumption here is that you have a lump sum option.)

My short answer to lump sum versus annuity is—no surprise—"It depends." I've recommended both options to my clients according to each person's particular situation. Since this decision is often irreversible, it's critical to weigh all the factors. For starters, let's look at the advantages and disadvantages of both options. (In question 16, I'll get into some specific numbers that should factor into your decision.)

My short answer to lump sum versus annuity is—no surprise—"It depends."

COMPARING A LUMP SUM PAYOUT TO AN ANNUITY BENEFIT	
Lump sum	**Annuity**
Advantages 1. Flexibility. You have immediate access to the money and can invest or spend it as you see fit. 2. Control. You manage the funds and can adapt your investment strategy yourself based on changing needs or market conditions. 3. Legacy. A lump sum can be left to heirs if you don't use all the funds during your lifetime. 4. Potential growth. If you invest wisely and take a reasonable distribution rate or work with a skilled retirement financial advisor, you could potentially grow your lump sum substantially.	Advantages 1. Steady income. The monthly payments provide a consistent and predictable monthly income for life, eliminating the risk of outliving your pension. 2. No market risk. Once you choose an annuity, market downturns won't impact the amount you receive each month. 3. Simplicity. You don't need to manage investments, reducing the potential for financial stress.
Disadvantages 1. Longevity risk. If you live longer than expected but didn't plan or invest accordingly, you'll run out of this pension portion of your retirement income in your later years. 2. Market risk. If you invest the lump sum and your portfolio performs poorly, it will adversely affect your retirement income. 3. Spending temptation. Having a large sum of money can sometimes lead to impulse purchases or poor financial decisions. 4. Management. Your lump sum will require management or oversight to ensure you're making the best decisions for the money.	Disadvantages 1. Inflation. Over time, the purchasing power of fixed annuity payments can erode if they aren't adjusted for inflation. I consider this to be a big disadvantage ... and many annuities don't keep up with inflation, despite what anyone may say. 2. Loss of control. Once you opt for an annuity, you lose access to the principal and can't take a lump sum payout for an unexpected need. 3. Potential loss of value. If you die shortly after starting the annuity, you will almost surely have received much less than if you had taken the lump sum (unless you have certain riders or joint life options). 4. Less potential for growth. Unlike investments, an annuity payment remains fixed unless it has specific features to adjust for inflation or market growth.

You get one shot at making the right decision.

It's important to understand the advantages and disadvantages here. You get one shot at making the right decision. Once you break that egg, there's no piecing the shell back together. So, choose carefully.

Question 16: What numbers should I consider when choosing between the lump sum and annuity options?

In addition to weighing the above advantages and disadvantages, it's important to take a look at some numbers: both the internal rate of return (IRR) and any cost-of-living adjustments (COLA) for your annuity.

In my experience, the **IRR** is *the* decisive factor in most cases. Basically, this is the annual rate of return your lump sum must earn in order to match your annuity payments over the same period. I've seen IRRs as low as 1% and as high as over 20%. If an annuity's payments equate to a high IRR, then the annuity is probably the better choice. But if your annuity provides a low rate of return, all things being equal, the lump sum looks favorable. For instance, if your annuity payout has an IRR of 20%, it would be hard to pass up that option, since it's highly unlikely you can beat that return investing the lump sum yourself. Likewise, if it's 1%, it would be hard not to take the lump sum.

The IRR is the decisive factor in most cases.

Calculating your IRR takes a little math. First, you need to know your life expectancy. (Hopefully, you came up with this in question 6.) Then, you need to know both your lump sum pension amount and your single life annuity amount. (For now, don't worry about which option you'll actually be choosing. You only need these amounts to calculate your IRR.) To make the calculation, find an annuity calculator online[13] and input the following figures:

13 "Internal Rate of Return (IRR) Calculator," https://www.calculator.net/irr-calculator.html; "Annuity Rate of Return Calculator," iqcalculators.com, https://iqcalculators.com/calculator/annuity-rate-of-return-calculator/.

1. For "present value," "starting principal," or "initial investment," enter your lump sum amount.
2. For "withdrawal amount" or "payment," enter your single life annual (or monthly) annuity amount.
3. Choose the "annual" or "monthly" time frame depending on what you input for number 2 above.
4. If there is a place to input an "ending amount" or "future value," insert zero.
5. For "length of annuity" or "period," enter your remaining life expectancy (it can be in either years or months, so long as you stay consistent).
6. Hit the "calculate" button to come up with your annuity's IRR.

ANNUITY IRR CALCULATOR			
Present value (Lump sum amount)	Annual annuity payment	Final value (Ending amount)	Length of annuity
$200,000	$15,000	$0	30 years
Calculate button	Annuity IRR	Total payments	
	6.30%	$450,000	

Armed with your IRR, you can compare it to your retirement portfolio's ten-year range of returns. I like to use my own All-Weather Retirement Portfolio, which is a blend of 70% equities and 30% bonds (more on this in questions 27 and 28).[14] For this blend, the ten-year range spans a high of 13.14% to a low of 1.41%, with an

14 This is a portfolio I've developed (and written an entire book about). I'm biased, of course, but I think it's the best retirement portfolio around for most people. You can order a copy at https://a.co/d/eMiTEnv

average rate of return of 7.11%.[15] Statistically, over the course of a hundred years, only five years will fall outside this range (which is what we call "95% confidence").

If your annuity's IRR is higher than the average rate of return for your retirement portfolio (in my case, 7.11%), as a rule, I recommend opting for the annuity. But if your IRR is less than the average of your portfolio minus 2.0% (in my case, 7.11 – 2 = 5.11%), I generally recommend taking the lump sum. And if your IRR is between the two (in my case, between 7.11% and 5.11%), then I suggest basing your decision mostly on all the other factors. That's not to say I don't also recommend weighing the other factors in all situations; I'd just put much more weight on them when your IRR is in between.

So, what do I recommend when using the sample numbers in the above calculator? Since the IRR of 6.30% is between 7.11% and 5.11%, that retiree could go either way—lump sum or annuity—based on whatever makes sense for them. Maybe they'd like a lump sum to remodel the house or pay off a big credit card balance (but only if they can still generate enough retirement income with what is left over!). Or maybe they'd worry about having to manage a lump sum and prefer the peace of mind that comes with an annuity.

The next critical number for you to consider is any **COLA** included in your pension. Inflation is one of the biggest financial storms that retirees have to weather. How many years do you hope to live in retirement? It's not uncommon to plan for 30 years, and I cannot overemphasize how important it is to plan for a rising cost of living to match. Do you remember the cost of a hamburger 30 years ago? A postage stamp? A car? What do you think those things are going to cost 30 years into the future? Probably a lot more than

15 As of October 25, 2023. And as stated before, past performance is never a guarantee of future performance.

today—and more than a monthly pension payment will cover if it's not adjusted for inflation each year.

Some pension plans' monthly payments are adjusted for inflation. Is yours? A lump sum distribution that's invested to keep pace with inflation has a chance to do so. If you're considering choosing the annuity, make sure it includes a COLA provision so that your payments will also have a chance to keep up with inflation. If that number is too low, however, then even an annuity with a COLA won't cut it. And with an annuity that has no COLA provision, your purchasing power will be blown away. This is a big deal and often overlooked.

Some pension plans' monthly payments are adjusted for inflation. Is yours?

Question 17: How do I evaluate my annuity options?

This question comes into play either when you don't have a lump sum option or when you've made the decision to go with the annuity option. As always, understanding the advantages and disadvantages of each annuity type is crucial in determining which one is right for you.

These are the three most common types of annuities:

- Single life
- Joint life (also called *joint and survivor life*)
- Period certain

I described these types briefly in question 14. Now, let's look at the advantages and disadvantages of each.

COMPARING ANNUITY TYPES

Single life	Joint life	Period certain
Advantages 1. Higher monthly payment. Because it is calculated based on one life instead of two, a single life annuity will always provide a higher monthly payout than a joint life annuity. 2. Potential higher total payout. The total payout will be higher with this type in the case of a retiree who lives much longer than their life expectancy or who outlives their spouse. 3. Simplicity. A single life annuity is straightforward, since there is no need to factor in a discount for a second person, as with a joint life annuity.	Advantages 1. Payments continue after the death of the retiree. For the joint annuitant (the surviving spouse), this option provides a financial safety net and peace of mind for the remainder of their life, since they won't have to worry about losing the pension income if the retiree dies first. 2. Potential higher total payout. In the case of a retiree who dies first but whose surviving spouse lives long, the total amount paid out will probably surpass what would be paid out by a single life annuity.	Advantages 1. Simplicity. It pays out for a certain period of time, so you'll know exactly what you're getting.
Disadvantages 1. No survivor benefits. To state the obvious, if the retiree dies prematurely (and what death isn't premature?), payments stop, and the surviving spouse receives nothing. (This is what happened to my client Donna.) 2. Potential low payout. Similarly, the total payout would be very low in the case of a retiree who dies soon after starting the payout, in essence losing most of what was earned over the years.	Disadvantages 1. Lower monthly payment. Since the payment amount is calculated based on two lives, the monthly payment is reduced relative to a single life annuity. This reduction in the monthly amount is the trade-off for gaining peace of mind for the surviving spouse. But remember, this benefit will be negated if the retiree's spouse dies first, leaving the retiree with a lower payment than if they'd chosen the single life option. 2. Divorce penalty. If the retiree and their spouse divorce, the lower payment remains. 3. Potential lower total payout. If the spouse dies first (or even soon after the retiree), the total payout will be less when compared to a single life annuity. 4. Complexity. Factors such as the age and health of the surviving annuitant can complicate the decision and the calculation of monthly benefits.	Disadvantages 1. Payments end after the designated time period. If you live longer than the certain period of time, you don't receive anything more after that date.

There are sometimes *variants* of the above annuity options, such as the following:

- **Life with period certain.** This pays for a single life or a certain time frame, whichever is longer. If this option is available, it's usually worth considering due to the small decrease in monthly payments from the single life annuity option.
- **Joint life with a percentage payout to the survivor.** This option pays a certain amount at first and then, if and when the retiree dies first, a certain percentage (e.g., 50% or 75%) of the retiree's payment to the survivor. By comparison, the initial payout is higher with this option than with the regular joint life option.
- **Joint life with period certain.** Rarely seen, it pays out to the last to die or for a certain time frame, whichever is longer.
- **Single (or joint) life with cash refund.** If the annuitant(s) die(s) before receiving back the total initial investment in the annuity, a lump sum equal to the difference is paid out to a beneficiary.

This is a lot of information to digest. But your decision can become a little easier when you keep this goal in mind: How can I (or we) maximize the probability that, no matter what happens, we will be comfortable financially?

Keep this goal in mind: How can we maximize the probability that, no matter what happens, we will be comfortable financially?

Here are a few examples:

- If you're single and want the maximum income, then single life makes the most sense.
- If you have a spouse, you also need to think about their financial well-being, especially if they're younger or in much better health. If losing you would devastate them financially, then either a joint annuity or a combination of life with period certain makes the most sense.
- If a surviving spouse would be fine without the pension income, then it's a judgment call. How's your health? If it's great (and you and your joint annuitant are about the same age), then the single life option may make the most sense. But if your health is just so-so (or your spouse is much healthier and/or younger than you), then the joint annuity option may make the most sense.

Now you can figure out which type of annuity is best for you.

Question 18: Is it true that I'll face a big tax hit if I take a lump sum payout from my pension?

To answer this question, I'll tell you a story …

"Randy, I'm no dummy," a soon-to-be client retorted when I offered to help him fill out his company's distribution form to collect his lump sum pension. He was an engineer, so a pretty smart guy, but I thought I could help, since this would be his first time filling out this particular form. Instead, he filled out the form himself, expecting to receive a $400,000 lump sum distribution from the pension administrator. But he got only $320,000. Why the difference? Turns out, he checked the wrong box on the form, asking for the lump sum to be sent directly to him. In that case, the law required his company to withhold 20% to cover any possible tax liability. To make matters worse, the $80,000 he *didn't* get was taxable, and since he was under age 59½, a 10% penalty would be applied. He came back to me almost in tears. "Randy, I'm such a dummy. Is there anything I can do to fix this?"

Fortunately, the answer was yes. There is a 60-day window to correct this mistake. (Note, that's 60 days, not two months. I've seen this detail mess up a few people.) But to make this fix, you must also be able to come up with the missing 20% yourself (in his case, $80,000). You'll eventually get it back as a refund from the IRS but not until after you file your year-end tax return. Fortunately, my client had $80,000 available to add to his $320,000 lump sum payout, and he immediately deposited the full $400,000 into a rollover IRA, as required. He was lucky he had the money and acted in time.

Here's the deal. When you take a lump sum payout from a pension plan, 401(k), 403(b), etc., the plan administrator is required to withhold 20% of the distribution (with a few exceptions). This mandatory withholding acts as a way to ensure Uncle Sam will receive any required taxes on your distribution amount, since lump sum distributions are typically taxable. But there are also a few exceptions that will allow you to avoid paying taxes on your lump sum. These include the following:

There are a few exceptions that will allow you to avoid paying taxes on your lump sum.

- A direct rollover into an IRA
- An indirect rollover into an IRA (60-day rule)

- Beneficiary distributions due to death
- After-tax distributions

The exception that applied to my client was the indirect IRA rollover (60-day rule).

When you fill out the lump sum distribution form correctly, your full lump sum amount will go directly to your IRA (or a check will be made out to the custodian of your IRA). You never want your pension administrator to cut the check directly to you—just ask my client!

The lesson here (as with a lot of what's discussed in this book): Beware of the 20% mandatory withholding and make sure you check the right box. Better yet, get someone who has filled out a form like this before—or many times before—to help you!

* * *

Pension plans might seem like a relic from your parents' generation, but maybe you're one of the folks who have one. If so, the decisions you make about the payouts can literally make or break your retirement. You might say pension decisions are like getting a tattoo: They're permanent, so you better think them through carefully. Whether you're choosing between a lump sum to gain control over the funds (and the responsibility that comes with it) or an annuity that provides steady income but locks you in, be sure to understand the internal rate of return and cost-of-living adjustments to make a decision you won't regret later.

The devil truly is in the details when assessing what option fits you best. Do you want single life payments (higher monthly income, but your spouse gets nothing when you're gone) or joint-and-survivor options (lower monthly payments, but your spouse won't be left out in the cold). Whatever you do, don't pretend you understand all the details if things get too complicated. Sometimes the smartest move is to admit you need a little guidance.

Now that we've navigated the pension maze, let's dive into the wonderful world of retirement accounts. The rules are just as complex, but many times with retirement accounts, you have more choices to match your specific needs.

Chapter 5

Retirement Accounts

Sorting out all your options can be tricky when it comes to tax-advantaged retirement accounts such as IRAs, 401(k)s, and all the others. For example, Mark, age 56, retired early and had already rolled over his 401(k) into a traditional IRA a year ago. Now, he faced a dilemma. He needed more monthly income but didn't want to pay the 10% penalty for making IRA withdrawals before age 59½. He also didn't want to go back to work. What could he do?

When we met, I explained to Mark and his wife, Janet, that they had some options to avoid the 10% penalty, but those options would involve some trade-offs. Janet was worried about getting into trouble with the IRS, so I reassured her that I'm a conservative tax strategist and that if there's no clear code section, tax court case, or regulation to hang my hat on, I simply won't go there. That seemed to ease her mind.

I went on to describe Internal Revenue Code section 72(t) and something called *SoSEPP*, which stands for "series of substantially equal periodic payments." Basically, this provision allows early withdrawals from a traditional IRA so long as they occur as equal annual, quarterly, or monthly payments. But there's one major drawback: You have to continue taking those same payments for five years or until you reach age 59½, *whichever is longer.* In Mark's case, that would be after age 61. "That's not a problem!" he beamed. "We will have plenty of other retirement income." So, I helped them set up a monthly distribution from his IRA based on the SoSEPP rules.

When I talked to Jim, age 55, he was also thinking about retiring and had already heard about the SoSEPP provisions. The majority of his retirement assets were in a seven-digit 401(k) at his current employer. Soon, he would need to start taking distributions from his retirement assets for income. He had already talked to four other advisors who had told him the same thing: Roll over your 401(k) into an IRA and then start taking SoSEPPs from the IRA.

With Jim, I thought to myself, the structured—and inflexible—payment amounts he'd be required to take for the next five years could become a real issue, since he didn't have other sources of retirement income like Mark did. As I explained Internal Revenue Code section 72(t) and the SoSEPP provision, I stressed the fact that his periodic payment amount would be locked in for five years and that if he ever needed to take a larger distribution for an emergency—or for any reason—the IRS would go back all the way to his very first payment and slap him with a penalty and interest for breaking the "substantially equal" nature of the payment. Jim's face turned into one of worry.

I then went on to tell him about a different, little-known Internal Revenue Code rule. Jim could keep his retirement assets in his 401(k) and, thanks to another 72(t) rule that only applies to people who retire between ages 55 and 59½, he could take either an ongoing or partial lump sum distribution without any penalty. This would leave him the flexibility to take out more later if he needed it. He was visually disturbed, asking, "Why didn't the other advisors tell me this?"

"I don't know. Maybe they aren't well-versed in the tax codes?

Or maybe they would make a commission if you were to move your 401(k) into an IRA?" I ventured.

You can see why it's important to understand the different types of retirement accounts, the different ways they are taxed (including the tax traps, which can reach as high as 25%), and the various exceptions. These tax-advantaged accounts are a great way for most people to save for retirement, but the distribution phase can be a little tricky. Read up and be prepared!

Question 19: If I'm still working, which type of IRA—traditional or Roth—should I contribute to?

Great question. First, let's remind ourselves of the differences between the two. Traditional IRAs and Roth IRAs are both tax-advantaged retirement savings accounts, and both have contribution limits depending on age. (For 2025, it was $7,000 for those aged 49 and under and $8,000 for those aged 50 and older.) But they also have some key differences, particularly in terms of tax treatment, eligibility, and withdrawal rules.

They have some key differences, particularly in terms of tax treatment, eligibility, and withdrawal rules.

Breaking Down the Key Differences

Tax Treatment

- **Traditional IRA.** Contributions are tax-deductible for the tax year of the contribution. You can also wait to contribute until the tax-filing deadline (generally April 15) for the previous tax year if you choose to do so. These contributions will reduce your taxable income (i.e., this is a before-tax IRA). However, withdrawals in retirement are taxed as ordinary income.

- **Roth IRA.** Contributions are made with after-tax dollars, meaning there's no tax deduction in the year of contribution. However, withdrawals in retirement are generally tax-free if the Roth IRA is five years old (otherwise it's taxed on the earnings portion) and you are over the age of 59½ (otherwise there's typically a 10% penalty on earnings for early withdrawal).

Income Eligibility

Which type of IRA you're allowed to contribute to depends on three factors: your filing status, your adjusted gross income, and whether you or your spouse has a retirement plan at work, such as a pension, 401(k), or Simplified Employee Pension (SEP). (Remember, you can only contribute to an IRA if you or your spouse has earned income.) Here are the 2025 eligibility tables.

TRADITIONAL IRA (if you have a retirement plan)		
Filing status	**Modified adjusted gross income (MAGI)**	**Deduction limit**
Single	$79,000 or less	Full deduction up to the amount of your contribution limit
	More than $79,000 but less than $89,000	Partial deduction
	$89,000 or more	No deduction
Married filing jointly	$126,000 or less	Full deduction up to the amount of your contribution limit
	More than $126,000 but less than $146,000	Partial deduction
	$146,000 or more	No deduction
Married filing separately	Less than $10,000	Partial deduction
	$10,000 or more	No deduction
Source: IRM Procedural Update, 11/13/2024 https://www.irs.gov/pub/foia/ig/spder/ts-21-1124-1129.pdf		

TRADITIONAL IRA (if you do <u>not</u> have a retirement plan)		
Filing status	**Modified adjusted gross income (MAGI)**	**Deduction limit**
Single, head of household, or qualifying widow(er)	Any amount	Full deduction up to the amount of your contribution limit
Married filing jointly with a spouse who is not covered by a plan at work	Any amount	Full deduction up to the amount of your contribution limit
Married filing jointly with a spouse who is covered by a plan at work	$236,000 or less	Full deduction up to the amount of your contribution limit
	More than $236,000 but less than $246,000	Partial deduction
	$246,000 or more	No deduction
Married filing separately with a spouse who is covered by a plan at work	Less than $10,000	Partial deduction
	$10,000 or more	No deduction
Source: IRM Procedural Update, 11/13/2024 https://www.irs.gov/pub/foia/ig/spder/ts-21-1124-1129.pdf		

ROTH IRA		
Filing status	**Modified adjusted gross income (MAGI)**	**Contribution limit**
Single	Any amount	Full deduction up to the amount of your contribution limit
	More than $150,000 but less than $165,000	Partial contribution
	$165,000 or more	Not eligible
Married filing jointly	$236,000 or less	$7,000
	More than $236,000 but less than $246,000	Partial contribution
	$246,000 or more	Not eligible
Married filing separately	Less than $10,000	Partial contribution
	$10,000 or more	Not eligible
Source: IRM Procedural Update, 11/13/2024 https://www.irs.gov/pub/foia/ig/spder/ts-21-1124-1129.pdf		

Withdrawal Rules

- **Traditional IRA.** You must start taking required minimum distributions (RMDs) at age 73 (75 if born in 1960 or later) whether you need the money or not. Miss these withdrawals, and they are subject to a 25% penalty. Early withdrawals (before age 59½) are also subject to a 10% penalty, although there are exceptions.[16] (The SoSEPP exception is the one that Mark availed himself of.)
- **Roth IRA.** There are no RMDs during the account owner's lifetime, allowing the account to grow tax-free indefinitely.

16 For the curious, the exceptions are listed under Internal Revenue Code section 72(t).

Contributions (but not earnings) can be withdrawn tax-free and penalty-free at any time. To withdraw earnings tax-free and penalty-free, the account must be at least five years old, and you must be 59½ or meet another qualifying condition (such as buying a first home).

Estate Planning

- **Traditional IRA.** Beneficiaries will owe taxes on any distributions they take.
- **Roth IRA.** Beneficiaries can take distributions tax-free.

What about After-Tax IRAs?

There are also what I call *after-tax IRAs.* (Technically, these are traditional IRAs with after-tax contributions.) This type of IRA is typically considered only by high-income earners who are not eligible for a traditional or Roth IRA. Unlike those that lower your taxable income in the year they're made, after-tax IRA contributions do not provide a tax break up front. Here's how they work and some considerations:

- **Nondeductible.** The main characteristic of after-tax IRAs is that they do not reduce your taxable income in the year you make the contribution, unlike the more common traditional IRAs. Contributions are made with money that has already been taxed.
- **Taxation upon withdrawal.** With an after-tax IRA, the portion of any withdrawal that represents the original after-tax contribution comes out tax-free, since those dollars were already taxed. But beware: Any subsequent earnings on after-tax contributions are taxed as ordinary income when withdrawn. If you also have a traditional pre-tax IRA, a portion of the distribution is considered as coming from

there. It gets very complicated, and if you aren't careful here, you may end up paying double taxes on the after-tax portion or penalties on what you should have claimed but didn't.

- **Conversion considerations.** After-tax contributions to traditional IRAs are often associated with a strategy known as a *backdoor Roth IRA conversion*. This strategy is used by individuals whose income exceeds the limits for direct Roth IRA contributions. They make after-tax contributions to a traditional IRA and then convert those contributions to a Roth IRA. Because the contributions were after-tax, the conversion is generally tax-free, except for any earnings that have accrued in the meantime.

What's the bottom line on after-tax IRAs? While I generally like tax-saving strategies, this one seems like it's trying to get around the limitation rule. It's also generally frowned upon by the IRS (or so I've been told), *especially* if there is very little time between the after-tax contribution and the conversion to Roth. So, if you're going to do a backdoor Roth, wait at least 60 days before converting.

I also generally don't recommend after-tax IRAs. Instead, you can set up a portfolio of exchange-traded funds (ETFs) or a no-load variable annuity and receive virtually the same benefit without the hassle (see question 31 for more on ETFs).

Which Should You Choose?

As for which type of IRA to contribute to, choosing between a traditional IRA and a Roth IRA, you probably won't be surprised to hear my usual reply: It depends. You should look at several factors: your current tax rate versus your expected tax rate in retirement, your income level, and your financial goals, including when you plan to retire and how you want to manage your tax liabilities.

My recommendation regarding which type of IRA to choose usually goes down this road:

1. Are you going to be in a *higher* tax bracket in the future when you take distributions as compared to today? If yes, then choose a Roth IRA.
2. Are you going to be in a *lower* tax bracket in the future when you take distributions as compared to today? If yes, then choose a traditional IRA.
3. And if you don't have a clue about your future tax bracket, are you currently in the 12% tax bracket or lower? If yes, choose a Roth IRA; otherwise, go with a traditional one.

Question 20: Once I'm retired, which IRA should I take distributions from?

The answer to this question is fairly simple and straightforward. (Of course, it also depends.) These are the factors to consider: your current tax bracket, whether you have to take a required minimum distribution (RMD) (you don't want to miss those), your income needs, and the amounts in each type of IRA and any other retirement accounts. My recommendations assume you have your retirement assets in only traditional and Roth IRAs, and they change if you're one of the few people who have after-tax IRA accounts. In all cases, you need a multiyear approach.

Here are my general guidelines:

1. First, take the RMD from a traditional IRA.
2. If that is not enough income to meet your needs, then take a larger distribution from your traditional IRA to bring your

taxable income up to the 12% tax bracket ceiling. This "locks in" these dollars in a low tax bracket.

3. If that's still not enough income, take the rest of what you need as a distribution from your Roth IRA. (If you have after-tax IRAs or other after-tax retirement accounts, take from those first instead.)

That's it.

Question 21: What options do I have at retirement for the funds in my 401(k), 457, or 403(b) plans?

When you retire, you have several options for what to do with the funds in your 401(k), 457, or 403(b) plans. These can be big-time decisions with a lifetime impact—and some options are irreversible. Below is a breakdown of the typical choices available to you.

1. Simply leave your funds in the plan and take your required minimum distributions (RMDs).

You can often leave your investments in your current plan if your account balance meets a minimum requirement. This option allows your money to continue growing tax deferred. If you are no longer working for the company where your retirement plan is located, then you'll have to take an RMD at a certain age (73 for those born in 1959 or earlier, 75 for those born in 1960 or later). These withdrawals are calculated using IRS Uniform Lifetime Tables (or if your spouse is more than 10 years younger, use joint life expectancy) and end-of-year account balance.

This choice makes sense if the retirement plan offers enough investment options to diversify the portfolio well and has low expense ratios. It can also make sense to leave your money there if you retire between the ages of 55 and 59½ (or with 457 plans, if you retire at any age) because of the more flexible, penalty-free distribution rules compared to IRAs.

2. Roll over the money.

- **Into an IRA.** Rolling over into an IRA can give you more control over your investment choices, better asset allocation, and potentially lower fees. There are no taxes due upon rolling it over, and the account will continue to grow tax deferred. Generally, because of the differences in the distribution rules, you don't want to do this if you retire between the ages of 55 and 59½. (Question 22 will go into much more detail about the rollover option.)
- **Into another employer's plan.** If you aren't fully retired and start a new job that also offers a retirement plan, you will probably have the option to roll over your previous plan into the new one. This usually only makes sense if the new plan has better options to diversify the portfolio and better expense ratios.

3. Withdraw the funds.

- **As a lump sum.** You can take out all your funds at once, but this is generally taxable as income and could push you into a higher tax bracket for the year you withdraw. Usually not a good option.
- **In periodic withdrawals.** Instead of taking everything out at once, you can choose to withdraw smaller amounts periodically, for example, monthly. If you have a 401(k) or a 403(b) and retire after age 55 (as opposed to after 59½ with an IRA), there

is no 10% early withdrawal penalty. With a 457 plan, you can pull out funds at any age after you retire. After age 59½ you need to weigh the benefits of leaving it in the plan or rolling it over to an IRA (see above).

- **By annuitization.** Some of these plans allow you to convert the funds into an annuity, which provides regular payments for life. This can be a way to ensure a steady income stream in retirement. The trade-off here is that annuities usually don't include cost-of-living adjustments. And as a general rule, once you start taking annuity payments, you can't undo your decision. So, make sure you understand the ins and outs of annuitization before choosing this option.

4. Convert the funds to a Roth IRA.

If you have pre-tax contributions in a traditional 401(k), 457, or 403(b), you might consider converting them to a Roth IRA. This involves paying taxes on the converted amount but allows for tax-free growth and withdrawals afterward. Taking this route is especially nice if you are in a lower tax bracket. Plus, Roth IRAs do not have minimum distribution requirements. (Again, see question 22 for more details.)

Each of the above options has tax implications and potential pros and cons, depending on factors such as your financial situation, tax bracket, and retirement goals. It's crucial to consider how each choice might impact your long-term financial health and tax situation. Consulting with a financial advisor who specializes in retirement issues can be particularly beneficial in navigating these decisions to maximize the effectiveness of your retirement portfolio (see chapter 10 on finding a good advisor).

Question 22: Should I roll over my 401(k), 403(b), or 457 retirement plan into an IRA?

This can be an important question once you retire. (Some retirement plans also allow for in-service rollovers once you reach a certain age and if you're still working.) Surprise, my answer is "It depends." Rolling over any of these employer-sponsored retirement plans into an IRA can have both advantages and disadvantages. The table on the next page provides an overview to help you weigh your options.

Here are my general rules of thumb to help you reach your own decision:

1. If you're under age 59½ and allowed to take distributions from your retirement plan without the 10% penalty, then leave your money in your retirement plan.
2. If you're under age 59½ but *not* allowed to take distributions without the penalty, then compare the investment options and the expenses on your retirement plan to those of an IRA. Many times, rolling over to an IRA makes the most financial sense.
3. If you're age 59½ or older, compare the investment options and the expenses on your retirement plan to those of an IRA. Again, many times, rolling over into an IRA makes the most financial sense.
4. If you are in the 12% tax bracket, consider converting your retirement plan into a Roth IRA, but convert no more than the amount needed to keep you from paying taxes above the 12% rate.

---

17 There are other exceptions that can be found in Internal Revenue Code section 72(t).

ROLLING OVER A RETIREMENT PLAN INTO AN IRA

Advantages

1. Broader investment choices. This can be a big one. Asset allocation, especially in the retirement plan distribution stage, is one, if not *the*, key factor in building an all-weather retirement portfolio. IRAs typically offer a wider range of investment asset classes than your retirement plan. They come in various forms, such as mutual funds, ETFs, and sometimes even real estate. This variety allows for a better (i.e., more return for the risk) retirement portfolio and a more personalized investment mix.
2. Potentially lower fees. IRAs may have lower administrative fees and expenses compared to some retirement plans, but be sure to compare the fees of your current retirement plan with those of potential IRAs before making the switch (see disadvantage 3 below, "Potentially higher fees and hidden costs").
3. Consolidation. If you have multiple retirement accounts, rolling them into a single IRA can simplify your finances by making it easier to manage your investments.
4. Estate planning benefits. IRAs often offer more flexibility in terms of estate planning compared to retirement plans. For example, IRAs allow for the naming of multiple and contingent beneficiaries.
5. Access to professional advice. Many retirement plans offer little to no professional advice for a person's specific situation. When you roll over into an IRA, usually it's with the help of a professional advisor. But beware of any front-end or back-end charges and be sure you understand fully how the advisor is getting compensated. (Hint: They are not working for free.) (See question 50 for more on advisor fees.)

Disadvantages

1. Protection from creditors. Retirement plans generally offer better protection against creditors under federal law than IRAs. And while IRAs do offer some protection, the level of protection can vary by state.
2. Loan options. Unlike most retirement plans, IRAs do not allow loans. If you anticipate needing to borrow from your retirement savings, this could be a significant drawback.
3. Potentially higher fees and hidden costs. IRAs may have higher administrative fees and expenses compared to some retirement plans. Again, it's important to compare the fees of your current retirement plans with those of potential IRAs. Some IRAs have back-end loads that charge you if you take out money within a certain time frame.
4. Required minimum distributions (RMDs). RMDs for IRAs start at age 73 (75 if you were born in 1960 or later), just like retirement plans. But if you are still working beyond this age and do not own 5% or more of the business you're employed by, you may be able to delay RMDs from your current employer's retirement plan. This option is not available with an IRA.
5. Early withdrawal penalties. Both retirement plans (generally) and IRAs impose penalties for withdrawals before age 59 ½. However, some 401(k) and 403(b) plans allow for penalty-free withdrawals starting at age 55 if you retire between the ages of 55 and 59 1/2,which is not an option with an IRA. And with governmental 457 plans, you can withdraw at any time after separation of service without an early withdrawal penalty. [17]
6. Rollover process. The process of rolling over your retirement plan into an IRA can be complex and might trigger tax implications if not done correctly. Direct rollovers are typically recommended to avoid automatic withholding, taxes, and penalties. A direct rollover means it goes directly from one custodian to the next without you ever taking possession of the money.

As with all such questions, before deciding whether to roll over, be sure to consider your individual financial situation, investment goals, and the specific features of your current retirement plan versus the IRA options available to you.

* * *

As we've seen throughout this chapter, retirement accounts are like a Swiss Army knife—incredibly useful tools, but you need to know which blade to use for which job. Are you dealing with the rigid structure of SoSEPP payments, trying to decide between traditional and Roth contributions, or figuring out what to do with that hefty 401(k) balance? Mark found his IRA solution by taking systematic withdrawals, while Jim discovered that sometimes the obvious advice (roll everything into an IRA) isn't the best advice.

When it comes to an IRA strategy, one size definitely does not fit all. Your age, tax bracket, income needs, and even your employer's specific plan features can dramatically change what makes sense for your situation. Don't let the complexity intimidate you but do respect it enough to either become well-versed in the rules yourself or work with someone who is. A wrong decision can cost you thousands in penalties and taxes—or worse, leave you scrambling for income when you should be enjoying your golden years.

Retirement accounts are often a big piece of the retirement income puzzle. To fill the gaps, you may also need to get creative and explore some other sources of income. Who knows, maybe taking on a meaningful new retirement job will prove even more rewarding than your previous big paycheck position. We'll review this and some more income options in the next chapter.

Chapter 6

Other Sources of Income

Tom walked into my office, head down and without a smile. He was 60 and hated his job. His boss was a jerk who seemed to live for making Tom's life miserable, and it was affecting his health. The problem was, Tom couldn't afford to retire yet, or so he thought. He was trying to find a new job, but as he put it, "Nobody wants to hire a 60-year-old who looks 75." It was true. Tom had aged considerably in the last two years and now looked much older than his 60 years.

Tom did need to keep working. I knew the numbers in his retirement portfolio wouldn't quite provide for the retirement he wanted if he just quit. We figured he needed a modest income source for about five more years. I asked Tom where he was looking for a new job, and he mentioned a lot of well-known companies in his field.

"Have you ever thought about working part-time or at a lower salary to fill in the gap?" I asked. He looked at me and sat a little straighter as I continued. "What about a not-for-profit? You could work for someone who can really use your skill set, make a big difference in people's lives, and earn enough to meet your retirement needs. In fact, you could afford to work that kind of job today. You wouldn't be making the money you do now, but it would get you out of your toxic environment and keep you on track with a solid plan for retirement."

Tom loved this idea. He ended up finding a full-time job at a not-for-profit. He even considers himself to be retired now because he loves what he's doing so much that it doesn't feel to him like he's working. Tom also feels like his life is meaningful because he's making a positive difference in many other people's lives.

And it all started with a conversation about other income …

Question 23: Should I work part-time after retiring?

Maybe. It depends on why you're asking the question.

Do you *need* to work part-time, like Tom did? "The best-laid plans of mice and men often go awry," as Scottish poet Robert Burns wrote long ago. Did you get laid off at age 62 when you planned on working to age 67 and now find yourself forced to retire before you're financially ready? In that case, a part-time job may be your best option.

> **Did you get laid off and find yourself forced to retire before you're financially ready?**

A part-time job may also come with employee benefits if you work enough hours. If you're under 65 and not yet qualified for Medicare, employer health insurance can be a big deal. But beware: If you're already collecting Social Security before reaching your full retirement age, earning too much can temporarily reduce your monthly benefits.

Sometimes your need to work is not quite so literal, but you nonetheless want more income. For instance, taking a part-time job can cover your "need" to take that once-in-a-lifetime dream vacation, upgrade your home, buy a new car, etc., that you hadn't originally budgeted for. This is an area where a financial advisor can help you find a way to spend without worry (or guilt).

Or do you *want* to work part-time even though you don't need the money? Maybe you have a secret passion or a dream job you never went after. Retirement can be your chance to explore those paths without the pressure of taking on a full-time gig or needing to earn a hefty paycheck. Maybe you've always wanted to work in a bookstore (that's me!), lead tours at a museum, or share your career expertise in a consulting role. Now's your chance to dive in and enjoy your job—just because you love it.

Maybe you have a secret passion or a dream job you never went after.

There are a lot of other good reasons to work part-time:

- **Staying active.** Working part-time helps you stay physically and mentally active, which is beneficial for your health. It's also good to have a reason to get up in the morning!
- **Being social.** When we retire, our social circles tend to shrink. A part-time job can help you maintain, and even increase, your social interaction.
- **Sharing your expertise.** You can be *the* difference for someone or for an organization. This is especially true for not-for-profits or a person just starting out in your field. The fourth quarter of your life (hopefully not overtime!) can be filled with significance. You can find fulfillment in roles that allow you to share your knowledge and skills with others, such as consulting or mentoring.

To answer this question for yourself, weigh your work-life balance. Consider how working part-time will affect your desired retirement lifestyle, including travel, hobbies, and time with family. Does the idea of working part-time spark a bit of excitement, or are you leaning toward full-on relaxation mode? Ultimately, it's about striking a balance that makes you happiest. And if you're married, be sure to talk over your thoughts and wishes with your spouse. They may even encourage you to work part-time ("Please, honey, get out of the house!") or may want to reserve some of your time for vacations ("Hey, these are supposed to be our retirement years!").

Lastly, whether it's due to a need or a want, a part-time job increases the probability of financial success for your retirement plan. That's because you'll gain more stability by adding a new source of retirement income.

Question 24: Should I consider taking out a reverse mortgage to generate retirement income?

If you watch any oldie show on TV (*Gunsmoke*, *Mayberry R.F.D.*, *Dragnet*, etc.), you're bound to see a lot of commercials singing the praises of reverse mortgages for every senior.

> I only recommend it as a last resort, a safety net of sorts.

A reverse mortgage is a type of home loan for homeowners, typically those 62 years of age or older. It allows you to convert a portion of your home equity into cash. Unlike a traditional home equity loan or second mortgage, loan repayment is not required until you leave your principal residence (perhaps moving into a nursing home or assisted living facility), sell the home, or pass away.

A reverse mortgage is simply a tool, and given the right situation, it can be a useful one. But I only recommend it as a last resort, a safety net of sorts. Here are some important factors to understand before picking up the reverse mortgage tool:

- **Payout methods.** You can choose how you want to receive the funds, which could be a lump sum, monthly payments, a line of credit, or a combination of these methods. Since most people are using this tool to make ends meet on their monthly budget, monthly payments usually make the most sense.
- **Interest costs.** Remember, the lending institution isn't doing this out of the goodness of its heart. It makes money through interest and fees. Interest on the borrowed amount accumulates over time. The loan balance grows as interest is added (hence the name *reverse mortgage*). Eventually, someone will have to pay that interest. However, reverse mortgages are non-recourse loans. If the accrued interest and current market conditions are not enough to pay off the principal and interest owed when the property is sold, your heirs will not be liable for any additional amount. But that also means your children might not inherit the family home if they can't afford to pay off the loan and will instead have to hand it over to the lender.
- **Fees and closing costs.** Regular mortgages come with fees and closing costs, and so do reverse mortgages, although often higher. If these costs are financed with the reverse mortgage itself, it may feel like you are not paying them—but trust me, you

If you're going to use a reverse mortgage, like your mama told you, you better shop around.

are. The fees can vary greatly, and most reverse mortgages are very expensive. So, if you're going to use a reverse mortgage, like your mama told you, you better shop around.

- **Homeowner costs.** You continue to own your home and are still responsible for paying property taxes, insurance, and maintenance and repair costs. If you're considering picking up the reverse mortgage tool, your budget is probably already tight, and these costs can be a real burden. That's why many people are better off selling their home to get away from these recurring monthly expenses.
- **Loan repayment.** The loan must be repaid when the last surviving borrower moves out of the home, sells the home, or passes away. If the home sells for more than you owe on the reverse mortgage, including fees, the surplus goes to you or your heirs. If the home sells for less than what's owed, the lender absorbs the loss, as most reverse mortgages are federally insured.
- **Eligibility.** To be eligible, you must be at least 62 years old (in most cases), own your home outright or have a low remaining mortgage balance, and live in the home as your primary residence. Additionally, you must meet financial eligibility criteria set by the lender.
- **Types.** The most common type is the Home Equity Conversion Mortgage (HECM)[18], which is federally insured and backed by the US Department of Housing and Urban Development (HUD). There are also proprietary reverse mortgages, which are private loans backed by the companies that develop them.

18 https://www.hud.gov/hud-partners/single-family-hecmhome

- **Counseling requirement.** Before obtaining an HECM, you must receive consumer information from HUD-approved counselors. This step is designed to ensure you understand the product, its implications, and the many potential risks and downsides.

Again, think of a reverse mortgage as a tool in the toolbox for those needing more income. With that said, you've worked much of your life to be debt-free. I like the idea of being debt-free, especially in retirement, including owning my home outright and knowing a bank can't take it away from me because something triggers me losing it. There are also a lot of costs involved in obtaining a reverse mortgage, so I only recommend it when every other resource has been explored. Of course, if you're at that point, go ahead and look into the details. Just don't go it alone. Visit with a financial advisor well-versed in the topic and your specific financial situation.

Question 25: Should I consider boosting my retirement portfolio earnings by adding high-risk, high-return investments?

I'm guessing you're talking about things such as private equity, hedge funds, and direct investments in start-ups or venture capital (such as your brilliant techie kid's internet company idea). Yes, these may offer the prospect of a higher return, but they come with a very high risk. These types of investments should only be considered if you have so much money you can watch it swirl

These types of investments should only be considered if you have so much money you can watch it swirl down the drain and not flinch.

down the drain and not flinch. If you're not in that category, my answer is simple: Avoid these sorts of investments.

- **Private equity.** Investments in private companies (not publicly traded) are considered illiquid, which is not something I recommend for retirees. This option is usually only available to accredited investors, anyway. Investors may have to wait several years for a return *on* their investment, and even longer for the return *of* their investment. Many times, this only comes around when a bigger company buys it or when it goes public through an initial public offering.
- **Direct investments in start-ups and venture capital funds.** Similar to private equity, these investments are in companies that are not publicly traded, often requiring a long-term commitment with uncertain liquidity events (a fancy term for a payout). Also not a good option for retirees.
- **Hedge funds.** This sort of investment usually comes with a heavy commission and a big salary paid to those running it. Many hedge funds have lockup periods during which investors cannot withdraw their money. Even after these periods, withdrawals may only be possible at specific intervals, usually annually on a certain date. Hedge funds are kind of like an exclusive club open only to a more sophisticated crowd of investors, such as wealthy individuals and institutions. They are riskier and more complex than your average mutual fund or ETF. So, it's a bit of a high-stakes game—and really not for most retirees.

It's a bit of a high-stakes game—and really not for most retirees.

I personally have never seen an average person make money in these sorts of investments. Of course, some people hit the jackpot in Vegas, but I've never met one of them, either.

Question 26: How should I tap into my investments beyond my retirement accounts and IRAs to provide another source of retirement income?

What we're talking about here is an after-tax portfolio of stocks, bonds, mutual funds, or ETFs beyond your three- to six-month cash reserve. Having investments like this outside your retirement accounts and IRAs adds some real versatility to your financial tool kit. That's because these accounts are superflexible. Unlike retirement accounts, there are no rules about when you can withdraw your money and no penalties or hoops to jump through.

When deciding how to use these funds, first you should consider your needs and intentions. Do you need money for debt reduction? A home improvement project? A long-dreamed-of vacation? Or to generate retirement income? When coordinated with your other goals, after-tax investments can be a good place to get the money.

Why? In a word, taxes.

On the one hand—and unlike tax-free distributions from some retirement accounts, such as a Roth IRA—the gain portion of the distributions from after-tax investments are subject to taxes. But on the other hand, these investment accounts may allow for some strategic tax moves.

For one, if you're taking payouts—be it one time, monthly, quarterly, annually, etc.—there are some big breaks versus payouts from pre-tax retirement accounts such as IRAs and 401(k)s. Let me explain. In a traditional retirement account, all distributions are taxed at ordinary income rates. But with after-tax investment accounts, the basis portion of a distribution is not taxed at all, since it's return of principal, which you already paid tax on. And the other portion of a distribution is taxed at capital gains rates, which is probably lower than your ordinary income tax rate. Not only that, if you're in a lower income bracket, capital gains can even be tax-free.

If you're taking payouts, there are some big breaks versus payouts from pre-tax retirement accounts.

For example, let's say that you invested $100,000 five years ago and that your investment account has risen to a current value of $200,000. (To simplify, we'll assume no capital gains distributions over those five years.) That means half the value of your account is your basis and half is your gain. Now you take a $50,000 distribution to pay down some debt and go on a nice vacation. At tax time, half your distribution ($25,000) is tax-free because it's return of principal. The other half ($25,000) is taxed at capital gains rates, which could be 0%, 15%, or 20% depending on your other taxable income and filing status (see the table below).

I don't know about you, but I like the idea of taking capital gains almost anytime it's in the zero bracket. And even if you owe 15% or 20% in capital gains taxes, it's likely that the tax will be less than if you had taken a distribution from your traditional IRA, which would be taxed at the typically higher ordinary income rate. You'll have to run the numbers for yourself, based on your particular situation.

2025 LONG-TERM CAPITAL GAINS RATES (TAXABLE INCOME)			
Filing status	**Taxable income**		
	0% rate	15% rate	20% rate
Single	\$0–\$48,350	\$48,351–\$533,400	\$533,400+
Married filing jointly	\$0–\$96,700	\$96,701–\$600,050	\$600,051+
Married filing separately	\$0–\$48,350	\$48,351–\$300,000	\$300,000+
Head of household	\$0–\$64,750	\$64,751–\$566,700	\$566,700+
Source: https://www.irs.gov/pub/irs-drop/rp-24-40.pdf			

Another tax strategy you can take advantage of here is called *tax loss harvesting*. Say it was a bad year and your investment account went down in value. You might decide to sell off some of those funds in order to claim a loss, which can offset other capital gains. Or you can use up to $3,000 against ordinary income to reduce your overall tax bill that year.

Another tax strategy you can take advantage of here is called tax loss harvesting.

My main point here is that after-tax investment accounts should be a part of your long-term retirement investment plan and coordinated with your expected taxable income. This may require a little work to figure out, but it's well worth the effort.

* * *

Chapter 6 reminds us that retirement income doesn't have to come only from traditional sources—and that thinking outside the box may lead to unexpected fulfillment, as with Tom, who found that shifting to work at a not-for-profit was just as good as retirement for him. It's all about understanding your "why." And what about some of the more complex income options? Reverse mortgages: Use only as a last resort, please. High-risk investments: Skip these unless you enjoy watching money disappear. The real gem might be your after-tax investment accounts, which offer flexibility and low taxation.

The bottom line? Having many income streams beyond traditional retirement investments gives you more flexibility and increases the probability you won't run out of money. And now that we've covered the many places where your retirement income might come from, it's time to shift gears and talk about safe ways to protect and grow what you've got.

Chapter 7

Investment Strategies

"The first thing I learned was to worry about the return of *my money instead of the return* on *my money."*
—Eddie Cantor

Mary had listened to commercials day after day about how investing in gold coins could make her rich with hardly any risk. The announcers warned that inflation was about to soar and described how gold coins were a great inflation hedge. She needed to move quickly, they said, and so she did. Mary invested $200,000 in the coins, which was a good chunk of her retirement savings. But in six months, Mary was stunned to learn that her coins were now worth only $130,000. She didn't understand why, and the account statements she received were confusing.

Mary came into our office looking for answers. "How can this be? They told me it was a safe investment." I helped her understand the statements and confirmed the bad news: The value of her investment had dropped by over a third in only half a year. This investment, and certainly the amount, was inappropriate for her both in terms of her goals and her risk tolerance. So many lessons to learn here: Don't listen to the hype, don't put too much in one asset class, don't lose focus on what you want your portfolio to do for you, etc.

Another client, Belva, came to me shortly after being widowed. Her husband handled the finances, and he had invested all their retirement money in one utility company. The utility company had a tremendous track record, paid a great dividend, and, well, utility companies are known for being "safe." On his deathbed, her husband told her never to sell that utility stock and she would be just fine. At that time, the stock was valued at a little over $19 a share.

I knew Belva wouldn't like what I was about to recommend, since it would go against her husband's last wishes. I explained to her that investing in just one stock creates a huge business risk and that she could avoid that risk by diversifying instead. It took some time, but Belva finally agreed to sell the stock and diversify her portfolio. As fate would have it, a few months later, the utility company filed for bankruptcy. Of course, I didn't have anything against that particular company—nor did I know it was about to file for bankruptcy (although Belva still thinks I have psychic abilities). Now, 25 years later, after surviving the bankruptcy, that utility still sells for about $19 a share.

In retirement, it's more important than ever to have a solid investment strategy—one you can trust to deliver inflation-proof income for the rest of your life. But caution is in order, especially when it comes to investing. If something sounds too good to be true, it almost certainly is neither good nor true. So, what investment strategies are the best for you?

Question 27: What should be my ultimate goal for retirement investing?

It can be tough at first to clarify financial goals for your retirement. But once you do, it's a lot easier to decide how to invest.

I start off by asking my clients, "How much return do you want on your investments?" I often get the answer, "As much as possible!" Then, when I follow up with the question, "And how much risk do you want to take?" I usually hear, "None!" I just smile in response. "So, your goal is to earn a big return with no risk? Me, too," I joke. "If you figure out how to reach that goal, please let me in on your secret!" This will usually get a laugh and remind my clients that every investment involves a trade-off between risk and return.

> "So, your goal is to earn a big return with no risk? Me, too."

Back in the real world, I propose a different goal for them to consider: *To maximize the probability that no matter what financial storms hit (and they surely will), I will have an inflation-proof, comfortable income for life.* After pondering my suggestion for a short time, most people agree to that goal. I've never had anyone say, "No, that's not what I want." Someday maybe, but not yet.

With this as the goal, "maximizing probabilities" becomes the heart of one's investment strategy. I know ... you probably want more than a high probability of success; you want a guarantee. But let me break it to you: There are no guarantees when it comes to investing. Financial markets are inherently volatile, and unforeseen events can potentially derail even the

> "Maximizing probabilities" becomes the heart of one's investment strategy.

most meticulously crafted plans. Maximizing probabilities is the ability to lower those risks effectively. By employing a probabilistic approach, you can anticipate and prepare for various scenarios, ensuring that your retirement portfolio remains resilient "no matter what financial storms hit."

Inflation is the biggest risk that most retirees don't plan for. It's an inevitable force that will gradually diminish the purchasing power of retirement funds. Over time, the cost of living rises, and savings may not stretch as far as we had anticipated. This is why "inflation-proof" is also at the heart of this investment strategy. The best way I've found to beat inflation is by allocating investments across diverse asset classes and employing tactics to outpace it. This will help ensure that your retirement investments will provide you with a "comfortable income for life."

If you choose this goal as well, then there are certain implications you'll have to accept. The first is that you'll need to diversify among various asset classes to give you the highest probability of success. That's because different asset classes react differently in different financial storms. Large cap growth, small cap value, core bonds, etc.—there's a certain diversified blend I've developed to achieve the goal. I call it The All-Weather Retirement Portfolio, and I've written an entire book about it. (I cover my portfolio's main features in question 28, coming up next.)

This leads to the second implication of our goal: When you diversify to achieve the goal, you will never hit home runs. Never. That's because trying to hit a home run by investing in the current hot stock runs the real risk of losing your entire investment. Buying a hot stock that grows tenfold in only five years simply doesn't happen when you invest in a well-diversified portfolio.

On the flip side (and the third implication): When you diversify to achieve the goal, you won't see a positive return every year. That's because you won't be investing only in "no-risk" investments, such as certificates of deposit (CDs) or US Treasury bonds, that offer a guaranteed return (before inflation is taken into account, that is). With an all-weather, diversified approach, your portfolio balance will fluctuate. Most years, you'll be up, but some years, you'll be down. Even in a very well-diversified portfolio, you should expect two, maybe three, years out of ten to show a negative return. (Wouldn't it be nice if I knew which years they will be!)

Even in a very well-diversified portfolio, you should expect two, maybe three, years out of ten to show a negative return.

Question 28: What are your recommendations for setting up my retirement portfolio?

As I introduced in question 27, I recommend what I call The All-Weather Retirement Portfolio for most retirees. This portfolio is a strategy designed to perform well under various economic conditions, intended to balance growth with protection against downturns. The inflation-adjusted income it aims to provide has been tested against real market conditions. When compared to every rolling 40-year timeframe since 1930, this portfolio is successful 98% of the time. For the other 2%, I apply my eight-year rule to protect against any exceptionally bad years during the first eight years of retirement. It's not guaranteed (nothing is when you consider inflation), but it passes a pretty strong test.

When compared to every rolling 40-year timeframe since 1930, this portfolio is successful 98% of the time.

Here are the key elements behind my all-weather strategy:

- **Diversification *among* asset classes.** The portfolio is spread across different asset classes, such as stocks and bonds, large companies and small, and US and international. This mix is intended to reduce the risk of big portfolio downturns by including different classes of investments that move differently in various economic scenarios. Sorry to say, but this also reduces the likelihood of any big upturns. Diversification works whether you want it to or not.
- **Diversification *within* asset classes.** No asset class leans too heavily on investments in any single company or industry sector. This way, if one company or sector performs poorly, the other parts of the portfolio can potentially offset these losses. Again, the trade-off here is that you give up the chance to hit a big home run.
- **The proper blend of asset classes.** You don't want simply to invest 10% of your portfolio in each of ten asset classes. It's like a recipe: Too much salt ruins the outcome. In a good portfolio recipe, a carefully tested blend of ingredients maximizes expected return and minimizes expected risk, especially on the downside. In your retirement years, when you're taking income, it's more important to control downside risk than when you're in the pre-retirement accumulation phase.
- **Preparation for the big one.** The portfolio aims to prepare you for almost any economic climate (that's why I call it all-weather). But what happens when that rare event hits, what we call a black swan, such as a tornado slamming into your house? (It can happen—it did to me, but I'll save my tornado story for another day.) Although my portfolio has been tested against

every storm since 1930, you may still experience a black swan event. It's impossible to create a portfolio that protects against an infinite number of possibilities, but my all-weather strategy was designed to maximize the probability of success.

- **Long-term focus.** This approach, since it's particularly aimed at retirement planning, emphasizes inflation protection and maintaining the portfolio for 40 years, which covers most retirees. That said, you can still expect two, maybe three, negative years out of ten. This portfolio is not for someone looking for quick profits.

This portfolio is not for someone looking for quick profits.

The essence of The All-Weather Retirement Portfolio is ensuring financial security throughout retirement, regardless of how the markets and the economic climate change over time.

Question 29: What are the biggest financial storms I might face, and what can I do to avoid them?

Your retirement portfolio, like the weather, is not going to enjoy only sunny days. Your investment will have to ride out some storms, and you need to be ready. One thing is for certain, after all: Investing involves taking risks. Some you can avoid completely, and some you can't. But you *can* protect yourself and reduce their impact. To do so, it helps to understand the types of risks. There are many, but these are my seven financial storms to prepare for:

1. **Business risk** refers to the risk you take when you invest heavily in one company or even one industry. If that business

(or sector) performs particularly badly or goes under, you could lose some or even all your money. Remember any of these bankruptcies: Enron, JCPenney, WorldCom, Lucent, Blockbuster, or Borders bookstores? Business risk applies especially to anyone who buys individual stocks or bonds, which is the reason I don't like investing in those (as I counseled my client Belva). Plus, it's an unnecessary risk. You can virtually eliminate business risk by investing in mutual funds or ETFs, which hold shares in hundreds if not thousands of businesses (see question 31 for more on these types of investments). If one or two companies in the fund go under, you may hardly feel it. The trade-off? Like I mentioned earlier, you give up the chance of hitting a home run by investing big in the next hot stock.

Your investment will have to ride out some storms, and you need to be ready.

2. **Market risk** is the chance of losing money on investments because of problems that impact the whole financial market. For example, if the stock market takes a dip, your retirement funds probably will too if they're invested in the market. This can be particularly concerning if you're relying on selling investments at a good price for your retirement income. You can't eliminate market risk entirely, but you can reduce it somewhat by diversifying across various markets: stocks and bonds, large companies and small, US and international, value-oriented and growth companies (see question 28). Even so, if the whole stock market is going down, then your equity portfolio will do the same.

3. **Inflation risk** describes the possibility that the money you've saved won't be worth enough due to the fact that the cost of living is always increasing. This seems to be the big risk that most retirees don't do a good job preparing for. It's also a risk that can hit retirees particularly hard when prices rise for food, medical costs, etc. If your retirement income doesn't keep up with inflation, you'll find it challenging to maintain your standard of living as you age. That's why it's important to have investments that grow at a rate that hedges against a bad period of inflation.
4. **Interest rate risk** involves changes in interest rates that can affect your investments and savings. If you have bonds and interest rates rise, the value of those bonds will decrease. If you're locked in to a long-term CD and interest rates rise, then you're stuck (unless you pay a penalty) with the lower-interest CD when you could have been earning higher interest with a newer CD. Also, if you plan on taking on debt (I hope not, I like being debt-free in retirement), higher interest rates could mean higher costs on variable loans.
5. **Longevity risk** is the risk of living longer than expected. This may be something that seems hard to get too worried about—unless you run out of money! How long do you want your money to last? Remember, you should *not* plan for your money to last only according to your life expectancy because that's just an average. According to the US census, there were over eighty thousand centenarians in 2020, and this was a 50% increase from the number of centenarians in 2010. That's why I like to plan to age 100 in order to reduce the risk that you'll outlive your investments. It's better to

have money at the end of your life than life at the end of your money (see question 6).

6. **Long-term care risk** is a scary one, since long-term care costs are going up much more quickly than the rate of inflation. Figures from 2024 indicate a national median cost of over $123,913 per year for a private room in a nursing home.[19] Although the average stay in a memory care facility may be only two to three years, people with Alzheimer's spend a much longer time there.[20] (See question 46 for a more thorough discussion of the threat posed by healthcare costs.) For now, I will say that it's a smart plan to buy long-term care insurance or self-insure by having enough money to cover the costs yourself if they arise.

Long-term care costs are going up much more quickly than the rate of inflation.

7. **Sequencing of return risk** refers to the sequence in which your investments perform well versus poorly—and it's especially important for retirees. That's because, over time, two equally funded portfolios may both average an 8% return even as one person is going broke and the other one isn't. How can this be? Say your investments go down in value at the beginning of retirement, and you have to sell off a large number of shares to provide your retirement income. That leaves you with fewer and fewer shares early in your retire-

19 Jeff Hoyt, "Nursing Home Costs in 2025," SeniorLiving.org, August 29, 2025, https://www.seniorliving.org/nursing-homes/costs/.

20 "What Is the Average Length of Stay in Memory Care?" SummerHouse Senior Living, September 27, 2022, https://www.summerhouseseniorliving.com/senior-living-blog/what-is-the-average-length-of-stay-in-memory-care/.

ment, which can significantly reduce the lifespan of your savings. On the other hand, say your investments do really well at the beginning of your retirement, and you sell off very few shares to cover your retirement income. This leaves you with many more shares still in your investment account and increases the lifespan of your savings. Sequencing of return risk is why it's so important to reduce your downside risk and to set a distribution rate that's sustainable even if your investments drop in the early years of your retirement.

Over time, two equally funded portfolios may both average an 8% return even as one person is going broke and the other one isn't.

The world of investing is indeed full of storms. You can avoid some, but you can't avoid them all. So having a solid investment strategy is like having a sturdy financial umbrella. It will keep you dry when that eventual storm does come.

Question 30: What's the appropriate asset allocation for a retiree?

Determining the appropriate asset allocation strategy—the "blend"—is pivotal in inflation-proof retirement investing. This involves striking the right balance between growth-oriented investments (such as stocks) and more conservative assets (such as bonds and cash equivalents). Generally, as someone ages, it's best to shift the blend toward bonds. For example, for those aged 60 to 65 and beginning to take retirement distributions, I suggest an equity/bond mix of 70/30; for those aged

70 to 75, a 60/40 blend; and for those over 85, a 40/60 blend. I also help my clients factor in their risk tolerance and personal goals.

On the **equity** side, I include the following asset classes:

- US large cap growth
- US large cap value
- US small cap value
- International
- Emerging markets

On the **bond** side, I diversify quite a bit also:

- Intermediate-term US bonds
- International bonds
- Emerging market debt
- High-yield bonds

This blend is designed to offer the highest probability of success for an inflation-adjusted income for life. (Again, for a much more detailed explanation, take a look at my book *The All-Weather Retirement Portfolio.*)

Beyond determining the right blend for you, a regular review and rebalancing are critical to ensure that your portfolio remains aligned with your investment objectives. An investment portfolio is not a static entity. Market conditions continually change. I like to review every quarter. If any one asset class is more or less than 2%

If any one asset class is more or less than 2% off from the target allocation, then I rebalance.

off from the target allocation, then I rebalance. That's it, four times a year. Of course, everyone's situation varies, so it's a good idea to get professional advice on the best asset allocation for you (see chapter 10 on how to find a great advisor).

So why not rebalance more often, you might ask, particularly if there's a big swing in the market? Simple: Investing for retirement requires patience and discipline, particularly when it comes to navigating those financial storms. A disciplined approach grounded in sound investment principles can help you stay the course and capitalize on the long-term success of the markets. Emotional decision-making, on the other hand, can—and usually does—lead to costly mistakes. When the stock market is down and things look bad, I've seen many an undisciplined investor decide, "I'm switching to cash until things settle down and I feel better. Then I'll get back into the stock market." Well, when do they feel better? When the market is back up, and by then, they missed the upside and end up worse off than if they'd stuck with their original plan. (A great book on this topic of behavioral finance is *Why Smart People Make Big Money Mistakes* by Gary Belsky, which is included among my recommended resources listed at the end of this book.)

It is important to remember that successful inflation-proof retirement investing is a journey, not a destination. It requires ongoing effort and discipline.

Question 31: What are mutual funds and exchange-traded funds (ETFs)? What are the advantages and disadvantages of each?

Mutual funds and ETFs are two popular investment options and the primary building blocks of a well-diversified portfolio. Why? Because they provide the first layer of diversification, otherwise known as eliminating business risk. That's the risk a business might go under and you lose all your money. People who buy individual stocks or bonds are very vulnerable to this risk (see question 29).

Most retirees prefer to avoid whatever investment risks they can reasonably eliminate. Investing in mutual funds or ETFs is one way to do this. Instead of owning a handful of individual stocks or bonds, why not own shares in hundreds if not thousands of companies? That way, when a few go under, they make up such a small percentage of your portfolio that you may not even feel it. So, what's the trade-off? You'll lose the chance to hit the big home run if you were to own stock in that one hot company. With your money in mutual funds and ETFs, it just can't happen. Is that a good trade-off? For the older crowd and retirees, I think so.

Instead of owning a handful of individual stocks or bonds, why not own shares in hundreds if not thousands of companies?

Mutual Funds

These come in two flavors: actively managed or passively managed. An actively managed fund has a professional manager who tries to earn you a better return than a comparable index (or basket of securities). For instance, perhaps the manager will try to beat the Standard & Poor's 500 index. To do so, of course, they'll have to earn returns that also overcome their expenses.

The other flavor is a passive index fund. This type of fund merely tries to mirror, rather than beat, a particular index. Since these funds aren't professionally managed, they typically have lower internal expenses and perform very close to their benchmark index.

Both flavors can have different types, or asset classes, that they try to beat or mirror. It could be stocks or bonds, large companies or small, US stocks or international stocks, or other assets.

Exchange-Traded Funds

As I imagine it, some smart person (much smarter than me) once asked something like, "How can we improve on the mutual fund model and design a fund that allows investors to avoid those pesky (and taxable) capital gain distributions?" Thus, ETFs were born. To avoid cash transactions that trigger capital gains distributions, the ETF issuer creates and redeems ETF shares, and this in-kind process avoids most, if not all, of the capital gains tax due from capital gain distributions. There are thousands of ETFs, and they are traded on an exchange, just like stocks.

What's my view about these two options? I've laid out the advantages and disadvantages of each in the table below. For many years, I bought institutional, no-load mutual funds. But now, because of lower expense ratios and avoidance of capital gain distributions taxation, I prefer ETFs.

COMPARING MUTUAL FUNDS AND ETFs	
Mutual Funds	**ETFs**
Advantages 1. Professional management (if it's an actively managed mutual fund). 2. Diversification. A single mutual fund can hold hundreds, if not thousands, of different securities, which helps spread out risk—but you lose the chance of finding, and investing heavily in, the next big stock. 3. Convenience. Just hand over your cash and let someone else manage it.	Advantages 1. Flexibility. You can buy and sell shares whenever the market is open (whereas mutual funds are bought and sold only at the end of the day). 2. Lower fees. ETFs are generally much cheaper than mutual funds because they're almost always passively managed. Mutual funds can be three to ten times more expensive—or even more. 3. Tax efficiency. ETFs rarely have those pesky, once-a-year capital gains distributions like mutual funds, so you won't have to pay capital gains taxes on those every year.
Disadvantages 1. Costs. Higher management fees, especially on actively managed funds, can really eat into your returns. Also, many funds have front-end or back-end sales charges. I tend to avoid these. 2. Capital gains distributions. This is a taxable distribution due to gains earned during trades within a mutual fund, even if those gains are automatically reinvested and the investor never touches the money. 3. Less control. You don't pick what you're invested in; the fund manager does. 4. Liquidity and timing. You can buy or sell your shares only at the end of the trading day.	Disadvantages 1. Transaction fees or a platform charge. You might have to pay a fee every time you buy or sell, or pay a one-time platform fee. These are generally very low, but they can still add up. 2. Daily market fluctuations. ETF prices can fluctuate during the day, so you always risk buying or selling on a dip in the day.

Question 32: Since I can't risk losing my retirement nest egg, why not put it only in guaranteed investments?

If you have a near heart attack whenever you see a drop in the value of your retirement portfolio, then, yes, guaranteed investments may be the best option for you. Investing in anything with even a low risk is probably not worth sacrificing your health.

That said, make sure you understand the trade-offs. At first blush, wanting to keep your money "safe" makes a ton of sense. Maybe you'll get lucky—there will be zero inflation, and you already have enough money saved up even if you live to 100. But you may want to think twice, since it's nearly certain you'll face some inflation during your retirement. Choosing only guaranteed investments does not come with a high probability that your retirement income will last the rest of your life when you have to keep bumping up your annual spending to match inflation.

Choosing only guaranteed investments does not come with a high probability that your retirement income will last the rest of your life.

When you say "guaranteed investments," you're probably talking about savings accounts, CDs, or government bonds. These are typically seen as low risk because they come with certain assurances, such as FDIC insurance (up to a certain amount) for savings accounts and CDs or the government's promise to pay you back for bonds. The appeal here is clear: You're much less likely to lose your principal when compared to more volatile investments such as stocks or ETFs.

But here's where inflation sneaks into the picture. Imagine inflation as a goblin who slowly eats away at the value of your money over time. Let's say inflation is at 4% per year. If your guaranteed investment is giving you a 2% return, you're actually losing purchasing power (in this example, 2% a year) because prices are rising faster than your investment is growing. In a way, you're "safely" losing money.

Now, I'm not recommending that you avoid guaranteed investments altogether. They have a solid place in a retirement plan, especially for short-term (under three years) goals and cash reserves (three to six months of your monthly expenses).

But remember what I've been saying throughout this chapter: Having your retirement savings invested in a well-diversified portfolio gives you the highest probability of success. Even so, you should expect to have two or three negative years out of ten. The key is having different types of investments that move up or down differently as the economy moves—think stocks versus bonds.

It's kind of like eating a balanced diet. You wouldn't want to eat only fruit (even though they're supergood for you) because then you'd miss out on other important nutrients. Similarly, mixing in different types of investments can give your portfolio a healthy balance, helping you achieve a reasonable expected return over time while also managing risks. You could also think of it like going to the doctor when you're sick. They'll prescribe something that will make you better. The remedy likely has some short-term side effects—most of them rare—but not taking it is more likely to result in adverse consequences.

Yes, it can be scary when it looks like you are losing money (or, as we financial planners say, the value of your portfolio has gone down temporarily). I recommend a strategy that maximizes the probabilities of success over time and works regardless of the economic situation. In retirement, stay conservative. (I know that's a subjective term.) On the risk-return graph, taking a little more short-term risk means quite a bit more expected return. This bump can really make a big difference during moderate to high inflationary times. Ultimately, it's up to you to decide which risks to take. Just be sure to consider the big picture, including the sneaky role of inflation, and how different investment types fit into your overall financial goals and risk tolerance.

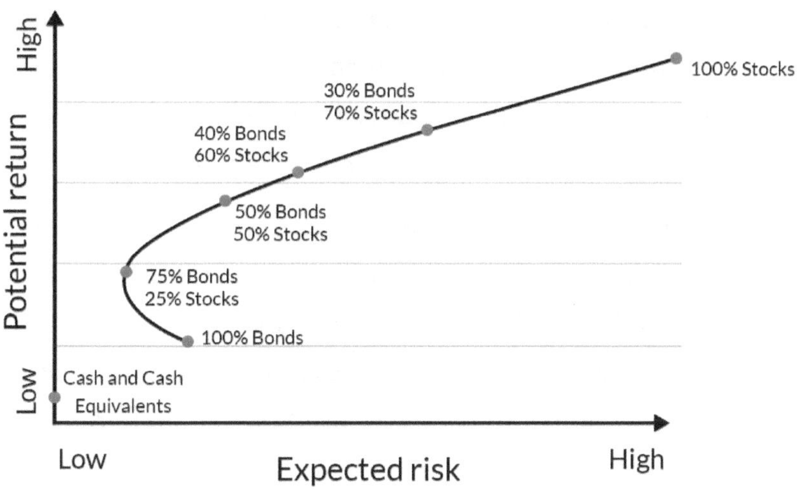

Question 33: What sort of help is available to help me manage my investments?

Using the right financial tools and resources can prove invaluable when you're crafting your investment strategy. Here are some of my recommendations on how you can tap into valuable insights, streamline your investment processes, and make informed decisions:

- **Professional financial advice.** Obviously, I'm biased, but working with a Certified Financial Planner® is my first recommendation to most retirees. Professionals can provide personalized advice, help navigate complex financial situations, and offer insights based on their expertise and experience. Find a CFP® who specializes in retirement, whose services are fee-only (that is, paid by you instead of financial product companies), and who serves as a fiduciary (that is, someone

Obviously, I'm biased, but working with a Certified Financial Planner® is my first recommendation to most retirees.

who by law must serve your interests first). These three qualifications alone will help you find a top advisor. (For a lot more on this topic, flip to chapter 10; or better yet, read my book *Five Steps to Finding a Financial Advisor You Can Trust.*)

- **Investment analysis software.** Sophisticated software is available to help you evaluate potential investments, conduct portfolio simulations, and assess risk-return profiles. These tools often incorporate advanced algorithms and data analytics to provide comprehensive insights and support informed decision-making (see the resources section at the end of this book for some specific suggestions).
- **Retirement planning applications.** Similarly, retirement planning applications can assist you in setting up a comprehensive retirement plan, tracking your progress, and adjusting as needed. These tools will also help you visualize your financial goals, analyze and compare various scenarios, and optimize your investment strategies accordingly. (I've also listed a few good ones in the resources section.)
- **Retirement planning courses.** I highly encourage self-education, if only so that you can ask intelligent questions of your professional advisor. Numerous educational institutions and online platforms offer comprehensive courses on retirement planning. Check out your local community college, adult ed courses at nearby universities, or even the library. You can learn a lot about investment strategies, tax planning, risk management, and estate planning.
- **Investment seminars and workshops.** These events offer invaluable opportunities to learn from industry experts, gain insights into current market trends, and network with like-

minded individuals. But be careful—many are mostly just platforms for "experts" to sell you their books and products. I'd skip any "free lunch" seminars offering meals, books, videos, or other up-front incentives.

> **I'd skip any "free lunch" seminars offering meals, books, videos, or other up-front incentives.**

I'd skip any "free lunch" seminars offering meals, books, videos, or other up-front incentives.

By staying informed, seeking professional guidance, and employing good financial tools and resources, you can enhance your chances of achieving your desired retirement outcome.

Question 34: Are you sure you can't help me find an investment with a big return and little risk?

Despite everything I might have said to them before, a few of my clients keep asking this question. I hear it at least as often as any other question, probably about once a week. High return with little to no risk: This is the elusive dream of many an investor. And, hey, if we investment advisors are so smart, we should know where to find it, no?

But I just keep repeating: In the real world, investments typically follow the golden rule of "higher risk, higher (potential) returns; lower risk, lower returns." So, if you stumble upon an investment or an advisor promising high returns with little or no risk, you might want to hold on to your wallet and just say no.

Remember what I've described above. It's a balanced approach with a mix of different assets that will help you manage risk while aiming for decent returns. Your job is to stick to your retirement goal and invest accordingly. And if you do find that magic money tree, remember to give me a call!

* * *

When it comes to retirement investment strategies, get-rich-quick schemes and "sure thing" investments are about as reliable as a teapot made of chocolate. Through the cautionary tales of Mary (gold coins aren't quite the inflation hedge the TV commercials promised) and Belva (never selling that "safe" utility stock may not be so safe after all), we're reminded that putting all your eggs in one basket is a recipe for scrambled finances. Instead, this chapter's core message is refreshingly straightforward: Your ultimate investment goal shouldn't be to find that big winner in the stock market but to maximize the probability of inflation-proof, comfortable income no matter what financial storms hit—and they will—during your retirement years.

The All-Weather Retirement Portfolio strategy that I've developed embraces the uncomfortable truth that successful retirement investing means accepting some trade-offs. You'll never be sharing exciting cocktail party stories about picking a stock that went through the roof. Instead—sorry to break it to you—you'll be commiserating with your fellow retirees about a couple of down years every decade. But by diversifying properly across different asset classes, rebalancing quarterly, and preparing for the seven major financial storms, you'll build a sturdy umbrella to stay safe and dry. It's all about remaining disciplined and remembering that investing for retirement is a marathon, not a sprint.

Now that you've got your investment strategy sorted out, it's time to tackle your tax strategy—because having a great portfolio is only half the battle if you're not tax-smart about how you withdraw from it.

Chapter 8

Tax Strategies

"A penny saved is worth two pennies earned, after tax."
—Randy L. Thurman

"Render unto Caesar what is Caesar's … but not any more than that."
—Matthew 22:21 (with Randy's commentary)

Ruth and Ruby are retired and widowed. They are lifelong friends, went to the same high school, were college roommates, live in the same neighborhood, and have two children each. They both had careers they enjoyed, in similar fields with similar incomes. They were married within a year of one another to men who worked in the same business. Their husbands both passed away suddenly, about a year apart. Their lives look like carbon copies, except for one thing: Ruby has more spendable retirement income—a lot more.

Let me explain. Both women receive about the same modest income from their pension plans and Social Security payments. Each one also has about $330,000 invested in her IRA and $330,000 outside her IRA. It's their after-tax income from those accounts where the two women's stories diverge: Ruth has $1,980 in spendable income from her investments every month, while Ruby has $2,887. That's about 45% more for Ruby, a difference of $907 cash, every single month! Since they both take a 5.25% distribution stream from their total portfolio, why the difference?

The answer is Ruby's smart tax strategies. She is able to get more out of her retirement income simply by taking her distributions from the right source. As a result, she pays less in taxes, leaving her with a higher amount of spendable income. This gives Ruby greater flexibility than Ruth to enjoy her retirement—to take trips to national parks, visit local antique shops (her favorite hobby), and even help her grandson pay for college.

No one likes to pay taxes, much less spend their golden years studying the intricacies of tax laws or keeping up with the changes in those laws every year. But the truth is, you will make dozens of critical money management choices every year, and many of them will have tax implications beyond how big the check you write to the US Treasury is or how large the tax refund you receive each year is. Understanding how your choices affect your taxes can make an enormous impact on how much spendable income you'll have for years to come. That, in turn, can make a huge difference in how well you can enjoy the worry-free retirement you've always dreamed of.

Question 35: When I'm retired, will I pay more or less in taxes?

Once you're retired and no longer working, you won't be earning any income and won't owe any taxes, right? Wrong. Even in retirement, several sources of income are taxable. This includes distributions from retirement plans, Social Security benefits, and even interest earned on your savings.

So, will you owe more or less? Short answer: probably less than before you were retired, but still more than you want to pay.

The long answer depends on several factors, such as the types of retirement income you have, your income level during retirement, and your tax filing status. In most cases, retirees pay less tax on their retirement income compared to their pre-retirement income. That's because most sources of retirement income are not subject to FICA tax (Social Security and Medicare), some sources of retirement income are tax-free, and some sources are taxed at the lower capital gains rates instead of the higher earned (ordinary) income rate.

Short answer: probably less than before you were retired, but still more than you want to pay.

Here's a quick breakdown of the different ways various sources of retirement income are taxed. (I go into more detail in question 36 next.)

Taxable income *(but without the FICA tax):*

- Traditional IRA distributions
- 401(k) distributions
- 403(b) distributions
- Pension income
- Systematic withdrawals from an annuity (as compared to annuitized payments)

Tax-free income:

- Roth IRAs and Roth 401(k)s (Roths must be five years old, and you must be at least age 59½)
- Return of principal (money that's already been taxed)
- Municipal bond interest (but beware of the Social Security tax—see question 37)

Income taxed at lower capital gains tax rates:

- Gains from a withdrawal/sale from an after-tax investment account
- Gains from a withdrawal/sale from an after-tax mutual fund or ETF
- Annual capital gains distributions in a mutual fund

Other income sources—such as annuities, life insurance, and part-time income—are taxed in a wide variety of ways that are too detailed to describe here.

It's important to know how your retirement income will be taxed because you'll be living on your after-tax cash flow. And we all want lots of cash flow and minimal taxes.

Question 36: How are my sources of retirement income taxed?

As outlined in question 35, different types of retirement income are taxed differently. Now let's take a more detailed look at the most common sources of retirement income and how they are typically taxed.

- **Social Security.** Social Security benefits are subject to federal income tax as ordinary income, but the amount you owe will depend on your provisional income. (Provisional income is your gross income plus tax-free interest plus 50% of your Social Security.) If this amount is between $32,000 and $44,000 for married filing jointly or between $25,000 and $34,000 for single, head of household, or married filing separately, then up to 50% of benefits are subject to taxation. Over that, up to 85% can be subject to taxation (see also question 37).

- **Pensions.** Pensions are typically taxable as ordinary income. But the tax treatment of pensions can vary depending on whether you made after-tax contributions to your pension plan during your working years. If you did, a portion of your pension income should be tax-free.
- **Traditional 401(k)s and IRAs.** Distributions from these traditional retirement investments are generally 100% taxable as ordinary income. And since the amount you withdraw from these accounts will be added to your other sources of income, these distributions may also push you into a higher tax bracket.
- **Roth 401(k)s and IRAs.** Contributions to these Roth accounts are made with after-tax dollars, which means qualified distributions are tax-free. (The Roth must be five years old, and to avoid penalties, you must be aged 59½ or older). This can provide an opportunity to withdraw more retirement income without incurring additional tax liability.
- **Annuities.** Annuities can have different tax treatments depending on their type and the funding source. Some annuities are purchased with pre-tax dollars (such as 403(b) s, also called *tax-sheltered annuities*), resulting in taxable distributions, while others may be funded with after-tax dollars (*nonqualified annuities*).

The taxation for a nonqualified annuity is a little tricky. If you "annuitize" (take monthly payments for a set period of time with zero value at the end of that time frame), then the percentage of the monthly payment that comes from after-tax contributions is considered return of principal and is tax-free. Say you put $100,000 into a nonqualified annuity and it has grown to $300,000. You annuitize and receive a steady monthly income of $3,000. Only $2,000 of that monthly income is taxable because the other $1,000 is return of principal. Alternatively, say you simply withdraw $3,000 out of that annuity from time to time but don't annuitize. In that case, the tax law says you must take the earnings first, so your full withdrawals will be taxable until you've withdrawn the first $200,000.

- **Tax-efficient mutual funds or ETFs.** Tax-efficient funds got their name because they're designed to minimize taxable distributions, making them a great investment option for after-tax retirement accounts. These funds typically generate less taxable income and capital gains. This is particularly true with ETFs, which rarely have capital gains distributions and are therefore extremely tax efficient.

> Tax-efficient funds are a great investment option for after-tax retirement accounts.

- **Municipal bonds.** Municipal bonds are issued by state and local governments and offer tax advantages. The interest earned from municipal bonds is generally exempt from federal income tax. Investing in municipal bonds can provide tax-free income, making them an attractive option for retirees looking to minimize taxes on their investment returns. However, be careful because this interest is included in the calculation of your modified adjusted gross income (MAGI) and can also trigger taxation of your Social Security benefits (see question 37).

- **Life insurance.** Certain types of life insurance policies, such as cash value life insurance, can provide tax benefits. The cash value component of these policies can grow on a tax-deferred basis. When you take money out, unlike annuities, you pull out your principal first, so that portion is tax-free. After that, many people borrow out of their policy because loans aren't taxable. At death, the loan is paid off with tax-free proceeds.
- **Part-time work.** Income from part-time work is generally taxable and subject to FICA. It's important to accurately report your income and pay any applicable taxes to avoid penalties or legal issues (and because it's the right thing to do). If you're currently collecting Social Security and are below your full retirement age, beware: There are heavy penalties if you exceed certain limits in earned income (see also question 37).

Understanding these details around how each type of retirement income is taxed can make a big difference in the amount of spendable income you have to live on once you've given Uncle Sam his share.

Question 37: How are my Social Security benefits taxed (or reduced)?

First, a little bit of history. Social Security benefits were originally exempt from federal income tax. Those were the days, my friend. But policymakers needed to find more taxes (what else is new?) and reasoned that, since other forms of retirement income were taxed, such as pensions, Social Security should be, too. Starting in 1984, if you exceeded a certain income level, up to 50% of your Social Security income could be taxed. In 1994, lawmakers were looking for more ways to bring in tax dollars, and they increased the amount to be taxed to 85%, again starting at a certain income level. The twist: They didn't tie these income levels to inflation, so they have not gone up since 1994. This means more and more of people's Social Security income gets taxed as the years go by.

More and more of people's Social Security income gets taxed as the years go by.

There are two primary situations in which your Social Security can be taxed or your benefit amount reduced. First, your benefits will be taxed, regardless of your age, once your provisional income exceeds the government-defined thresholds. This also depends on your filing status (see table below). Second, your benefits will be taxed if you begin receiving them before you reach your full retirement age (FRA) *and* you receive wages (i.e., earned income) over a certain threshold amount (see below). Your benefits will also be reduced if you're over that threshold, although you'll eventually receive the benefits back once you hit your FRA, but they'll be spread over your life expectancy.

First, let's look more carefully at the income thresholds and the amount of your Social Security income that will be taxed.

TAXES ON SOCIAL SECURITY INCOME		
Tax filing status	**Provisional income thresholds**	**Amount of Social Security income subject to taxation**
Married filing jointly	Under $32,000	0%
	$32,000–$44,000	Up to 50%
	Over $44,000	Up to 85%
Single, head of household, qualifying widow(er), married filing separately, and living apart from spouse	Under $25,000	0%
	$25,000–$34,000	Up to 50%
	Over $34,000	Up to 85%
Married filing separately and lived with spouse during year	Over $0	85%
Source: IRS Publication 915 https://www.irs.gov/publications/p915		

As I've said before, tax laws aren't necessarily fair. Think about it. Up to 85% of your Social Security income can be taxed even though you already paid income tax on half the amount (or all of it if you're self-employed) that went into the Social Security system back when you earned it. One could argue that paying taxes on those funds amounts to double taxation. And your so-called tax-free municipal bonds can also trigger additional taxation.

Next, let's look at how taxes on Social Security benefits relate to your FRA.

If you start taking Social Security before your FRA, your benefits will be reduced by $1 for every $2 in wages (i.e., earned income) you make over $23,400. That's kind of like a 50% tax on any earnings above the threshold. This eases a bit in the year you reach your FRA. In that year, Social Security benefits are reduced by $1 for every $3 over the earning cap of $62,160.[21] This is called the *special earnings limit rule*,[22] although it doesn't sound so special to me! (See also question 10.)

Technically, this reduction of benefits is not a tax because the reduction will be added back into your monthly Social Security benefit amount, amortized over your life expectancy, once you reach your FRA. But I'm calling it taxation, since it takes away from your benefits and in essence taxes your earned income once you reach a certain level.

> There can be real tax consequences for those whose retirement income, including Social Security, goes over certain government limits, even just barely.

The important thing to know is that there can be real tax consequences for those whose retirement income, including Social Security, goes over certain government limits, even just barely. That's why careful planning is important in order to maximize your retirement income without needlessly paying more taxes.

Question 38: When am I allowed to start taking money out of my retirement plans without a penalty?

It depends, based on whether it's an IRA, 401(k), 403(b), or governmental 457 plan. Let's look at each.

21 These are the earnings caps for the 2025 tax year.

22 "Special Earnings Limit Rule," Social Security Administration, accessed September 9, 2025, https://www.ssa.gov/benefits/retirement/planner/rule.html.

Traditional IRA

The general rule is that you must be age 59½ before taking penalty-free distributions. But, surprise, there are exceptions:

- **Series of Substantially Equal Periodic Payments (SoSEPP).** This is the one I see most often, in cases where someone wants to (or must) retire early. (Remember my clients Mark and Jim, from chapter 5?) It's sometimes called a *72(t) distribution* because it can be found under Internal Revenue Code section 72(t). This code section says you can take penalty-free early withdrawals of substantially equal periodic payments based on your life expectancy so long as this is done in a strict, calculated way. You must continue payments in this manner for five years or until you reach age 59½, *whichever is longer.* Example: If you start taking payments at age 58, they must continue in an equal amount until age 63 (i.e., for five years). After that time frame is up, you can do anything you want without penalty (see also question 19).

The general rule is that you must be 59½. But, surprise, there are exceptions.

- **First-time home purchase.** You can withdraw up to $10,000 (lifetime limit) from your IRA to buy, build, or rebuild a first home for yourself, your spouse, a child, a grandchild, or a parent without penalty. This is a one-time exemption.
- **Qualified higher education expenses.** IRA distributions used to pay for qualified higher education expenses for yourself, your spouse, or your dependents are exempt from the early withdrawal penalty.

- **Unreimbursed medical expenses.** If you have medical expenses that exceed a certain percentage of your adjusted gross income, you can take penalty-free withdrawals to cover those expenses.
- **Health insurance premiums during unemployment.** If you are unemployed and have received unemployment compensation for twelve consecutive weeks, you can take penalty-free withdrawals to pay for health insurance premiums.
- **Disability.** If you become disabled before age 59½ and are unable to engage in any substantial gainful activity, you can withdraw IRA funds without penalty.
- **Birth or adoption of a child.** You can withdraw up to $5,000 without penalty for costs associated with the birth or legal adoption of a child.

Roth IRA

If you have had a Roth for five years, you can take the proceeds out tax-free. However, if you take money out before age 59½, the portion that comes from earnings (but not the portion from principal) will cost you a 10% penalty.

401(k) and 403(b)

Again, the general rule is that you must be aged 59½. Most plans include hardship withdrawals for special situations specific to the plan. The big exception is the rule of 55. The rule of 55 states that if you leave your job during or after the year you turn 55, you will be eligible to take penalty-free withdrawals from your 401(k) or 403(b) plan. However, this rule only applies to the 401(k) or 403(b) associated with your most recent employer. Tax tip: If you are between the ages of 55 and 59½, you generally don't want to roll your employer's plan into an IRA. Why? IRAs don't have the rule of 55, and any distributions are subject to the 10% penalty.

Governmental 457 Plan

This one has no early withdrawal penalty. One of the key features of a governmental 457(b) plan is that it does not hit you with the 10% early withdrawal penalty that applies to other retirement plans, such as 401(k)s and IRAs. This means you can take distributions from your 457(b) plan when you retire or leave your job, regardless of your age, without incurring a 10% penalty.

Question 39: When am I required to take money out of my retirement plans to avoid a tax penalty, and how much do I have to take out?

Once you're retired, the government probably figures you've delayed paying taxes long enough on the money in your tax-deferred retirement accounts. The purpose of those tax breaks, after all, was to help prepare you for retirement. That's why you're required by law to take a minimum distribution from those retirement accounts and IRAs beginning at a specific age. The age at which this required minimum distribution (RMD) kicks in depends on your birth year. The table below lists the general rules of when you have to begin your RMD.

RMD BEGINNING AGES	
Birth year	**Age**
7/1/1949 to 1950	72
1951 to 1959	73
1960 or later	75

One exception to the RMD year applies to 401(k), profit-sharing, 403(b), or other defined-contribution plans. If you continue working full-time past your RMD year and you're not a 5% owner of the business with the retirement plan, you can delay distributions until you retire. Technically, you can delay the first distribution to April 1 of the year following the year you reach the RMD beginning age. But if you do, you must take the second distribution by December 31 of that same year. Remember, though, that for tax purposes, taking two distributions in one year is generally not good, since the second distribution is taxed at your highest marginal tax bracket at the time.

Another tax tip: If you're going to report a large income in your RMD year but little or much less income in the year after, it makes sense to delay your first distribution to the following tax year (but before the April 1 deadline), since it will be taxed at a lower rate.

So, how much do you have to take out? For most people, that number is calculated for you by the retirement plan custodian. It's based on the retirement account's value on December 31 of the year before you begin the RMD. That number is then divided by a uniform life expectancy,[23] married or not, provided by the IRS, which works out to be about 4% the first year (unless you're married to someone more than ten years younger—then divide by your actual joint life

23 Information on life expectancy can be found on the IRS website at https://www.irs.gov/publications/p590b#en_US_2022_publink100089977.

expectancy, provided in IRS publication 590-B).

The penalty for not taking your RMD on time is a whopping 25% of the required amount. So, you don't want to miss that deadline! Just ask Tim, who became my client at age 72. Born in June, he had hit his RMD date two years earlier at age 70½ (this age has recently been changed to 73 or 75 depending on birth year). He had a large IRA but didn't need the money, so he decided not to take a distribution. Big mess-up. He had to pay a big penalty for missing the two required distribution years. That 25% is a lot to pay for an honest, easy-to-make mistake.

The penalty for not taking your RMD on time is a whopping 25% of the required amount.

Question 40: What tax land mines do I need to watch out for?

There are *so* many tax land mines, and some could cost you a small fortune if you step on them. Of course, some could also be considered tax strategies. Either way, these change every year, so it's best to work with a tax professional. I'm not talking about someone who simply prepares your taxes but someone who offers proactive tax strategies.

I have listed the top ten most common and costly tax land mines for retirees:

1. **Not taking your required minimum distribution.** Miss your RMD, and it's a 25% penalty. Brutal (see question 39 for the details).

2. **Taking your 401(k), 403(b), or other defined-contribution plan rollover directly to you.** If you have the plan

administrator cut a rollover check directly to you (instead of the IRA custodian), the administrator is required to withhold 20%. You can always "fix" this problem (but it must be within 60 days) by placing the funds into the rollover IRA and making up the 20% difference from your cash or other investment accounts. But then you have to wait for a refund, and who wants (or can) do that? (See also question 18.)

3. **Filing under the wrong status.** Make sure you file under the correct status (single, married filing jointly, qualifying surviving spouse, etc.). Some filing statuses allow you to use a higher standard deduction, which translates to less taxable income. Here are a few common examples that can increase your standard deduction by thousands of dollars:
   - If you qualify as a caregiver for a family member, file as head of household instead of single.
   - If you get married, even as late as December 31, file as married filing jointly, since the IRS looks at your marital status on December 31.
   - If your spouse passed away during that year, file as married filing jointly.
4. **Not claiming your Social Security as income.** Depending on your other taxable income and filing status, up to 85% of your Social Security income can be counted as taxable income. This often catches retirees by surprise (see also question 37).
5. **Not claiming gains on the sale of property or investments.** When you sell property or investments for a gain, you are subject to capital gains tax. Not claiming gains is a

big boo-boo. Not only will you owe the unpaid taxes, but you'll also have to pay interest and even penalties. If you have held the asset for over a year, gains are taxed at the long-term rate, which is much lower. Gains from assets held for under a year are taxed as short-term, which is a higher rate. Tax tip: Consider delaying selling property or investments until after one year if you are close to that threshold.

6. **Taking IRA distributions too soon.** If you take money out of IRAs before age 59½, you will owe a 10% penalty. There are exceptions, but beware. This includes Roth IRAs (see also question 38).

7. **Underestimating taxable income and not withholding enough taxes.** Now that you don't have an employer withholding taxes from your paychecks, that's your job. You've got to make sure you anticipate all your taxable income and withhold enough taxes throughout the year so that the IRS won't penalize you for underpaying. That could be through estimated payments or withholding by various income sources. There are some safe harbor rules, meaning if you follow either of them, they generally won't penalize you for underpaying throughout the year:

   You've got to make sure you anticipate all your taxable income and withhold enough taxes throughout the year so that the IRS won't penalize you for underpaying.

   - You pay at least 90% of the tax you owe for the current year or 100% of the tax you owed for the previous tax year.

- You owe less than $1,000 in tax after subtracting withholdings and credits.

The rule is slightly different for high-income taxpayers. If the adjusted gross income (AGI) on your previous year's tax return was over $150,000 (or over $75,000 for single or married filing separately), you must pay the lower of 90% of the tax you owe for the current year or 110% of the tax you owed for the previous year.

8. **Missing the earned income credit (EIC).** There are millions of people at the lower taxable income level who are eligible for this credit. According to the IRS, 25% fail to claim it. If this is you, do you think the IRS will track you down to let you know you could have paid fewer taxes? I doubt it. The EIC is a bit unusual in that it is a refundable tax credit, not a deduction. The credit can be as high as $7,430. The rules can be tricky because the credit depends on marital status, income, family size, etc. If you missed claiming the EIC in previous years, you can go back and claim the credit for the three previous years.

9. **Not paying taxes on capital gains distributions from mutual funds in taxable accounts.** Usually once per year, mutual funds will distribute their capital gains. Even if you automatically reinvest those gains and never really see them, you still must pay taxes. (This only applies to taxable accounts.) Know that these gains exist and can be large, even when the account's value is down. Most times, these gains are reported on a 1099-B issued to you by the custodian at the end of January, but a call to your custodian at the end of December will get you the numbers earlier. Tax tip: Better to invest in ETFs that rarely have capital gains distributions (see question 31).

10. **Having your tax-free municipal bonds trigger your Social Security taxation.** The calculation for if, and how much of, your Social Security is taxed includes any tax-free municipal bond interest. In other words, municipal bond interest can trigger taxation of your Social Security benefits when they wouldn't otherwise have been taxed. If you're in this situation, many times you're better off with taxable bonds (which, all things being equal, pay more interest) or, if you don't need the income, a tax-sensitive ETF portfolio or tax-deferred vehicle (see question 36).

There you have it, my top ten tax land mines for retirees.

FINDING THE RIGHT TAX ADVISOR FOR YOUR RETIREMENT

You don't just need a tax preparer; you also need a tax advisor. Finding the right tax advisor for your retirement is essential. A knowledgeable tax advisor can help you navigate the complex world of income taxation, identify tax-saving opportunities, and build a tax-efficient retirement plan.

When looking for a tax advisor, consider their experience, credentials, and whether they specialize in retirement planning. Remember, a good tax advisor is both a financial partner who can give you tax strategies and a guide to a secure retirement.

Question 41: Are there some general guidelines I can apply to make better tax decisions for my retirement?

Applying the right strategies can help you land within that narrow margin between paying too much tax and paying less than the law requires. The trick is to lay some ground rules for smart decisions. Over the years, I've developed a list I call Randy's Rules of Tax Decisions. Below are a few of those rules that are particularly relevant for retirees. Think of them as a filter you can use to evaluate your options and the impact your choices will have on your tax liability.

Rule 1. Income is good (even if it's taxed).

There is not a year that goes by that I don't hear someone say something like, "I don't want the income; it will put me in a higher tax bracket." This only makes sense if you don't understand tax brackets and how they're applied to income. It's true that the percentage of income you pay in taxes increases as you move into a higher tax bracket—but remember, the higher percentage applies only to the portion of income that falls within that higher bracket. All the income that falls within the limits for the lower tax bracket will still be taxed at the lower rate. And no matter what tax bracket you're in, except in very rare circumstances, you will get to keep most of what you earn. So, if you find yourself with the opportunity—or the desire—to engage in some paid work during retirement, go for it. (For one exception to this advice, see questions 10 and 11.)

Rule 2. It's better to pay a dollar of tax tomorrow than today.

Tax deferral is usually good. Some people would disagree with me on this: "I just want to pay my taxes and get it over with." But think about it—if you can pay at some later date, rather than now, it means you'll have those dollars working for you during the time they're in your account instead of Uncle Sam's (so long as you don't incur penalties or interest because you've delayed paying, that is). There are exceptions here. For example, if you are in a low tax bracket now and expect to be in a high tax bracket later, it might make sense to pay at the lower rate now. Also, there might be some situations when it makes sense to convert traditional IRAs to Roth IRAs and pay the tax now, but that takes a complicated analysis beyond the scope of this book.

If you can pay at some later date, rather than now, it means you'll have those dollars working for you.

Rule 3. When it comes to owing taxes, some forms of income, or cash flow, are better than others.

Different types of income and distributions are taxed differently, and the amount of taxes you owe will depend on your situation. It makes sense to take money first from a source that's subject to the least amount of tax. This allows you to defer paying taxes until some later date (see also rule 2).

Take money first from a source that's subject to the least amount of tax.

Here's my general recommendation on which types of income to take first:

1. Tax-free dollars (e.g., money held in a Roth IRA)
2. Long-term capital gains (e.g., investments you've held for a year or more, which are taxed at a lower rate than ordinary income)
3. Ordinary income (e.g., taxable income from investments, such as dividends and interest, that is taxed at a higher rate)

Rule 4. Tax penalties and interest are bad.

As I said above, paying taxes tomorrow is better than paying them today—to a point. You don't want to underpay your estimated taxes during the year such that you must pay additional penalties and interest when April 15 rolls around. Those added costs can really add up. Make sure the proper tax amounts are withheld from your paycheck, pension, or distributions from investments. The rules are more complicated than I can cover here, but rest assured, there's always a safe harbor amount you can pay to ensure you won't have to pay penalties and interest (see also question 40). Your tax professional should be able to determine what that amount is for you.

Question 42: Do you have any other tax tips to help me reduce my taxes even more?

As I hope you've learned from the other questions in this chapter, tax planning is an essential component of retirement planning. Here are a few more tax-saving tips, not just about minimizing your taxes when you file each year but also about developing a tax strategy for the long term. From deductions to income distribution strategies to tax-efficient investing, there's a lot to consider. But remember, there's no one-size-fits-all solution. Your tax planning strategy should align with your financial goals, risk tolerance, and personal circumstances.

- **Deductions** are a retiree's best friend. They reduce your taxable income, which in turn reduces your tax liability. That's why it's crucial not to overlook the wide range of deductions available for retirees, from medical expenses to mortgage interest. Keeping great records of your expenses throughout the year is the first step in ensuring you can take advantage of all your deductions. This may seem arduous, but believe me, it's worth it. Consider using financial software, a good old-fashioned spreadsheet, or an organized filing system to record your financial transactions—the more detailed, the better. Without detailed records, you won't be able to claim all your potential deductions.

It's crucial not to overlook the wide range of deductions available for retirees.

- **Tax credits** directly reduce the amount of tax you owe dollar for dollar, unlike deductions, which only lower your taxable income. For instance, the nonrefundable credit for the elderly or disabled offers up to $7,500 for qualifying seniors, while state-specific property tax relief programs provide additional savings on housing costs. Early retirees not yet eligible for Medicare may benefit from the premium tax credit to reduce health insurance expenses. Energy efficiency credits, while they last, help lower both tax liability and ongoing utility costs.

- **Charitable giving** is not only a great way to support causes you care about, but it can also provide significant tax savings. When you donate to a qualified charitable organization, you can deduct your donation amount if you itemize. Consider donating appreciated assets such as stocks or real estate. By doing this, you avoid paying capital gains tax on the appreciation and still get to deduct the asset's full market value. It's a win-win situation—you help a worthy cause *and* save on taxes!

Consider donating appreciated assets such as stocks or real estate.

Once you hit age 70½, you can also send up to $108,000 (that's the 2025 limit) from one of your retirement accounts directly to a charity as a qualified charitable distribution (QCD). By doing this, you won't have to claim your RMD as income, thereby lowering your taxable income. While you can't also deduct it as a donation, it will reduce your taxes. And it's a great form of charitable giving for people who don't itemize.

The IRS also allows you to take an immediate tax deduction when you set up a charitable remainder trust (CRT). Here, you donate a highly appreciated asset to the trust, and you are allowed to receive income for a period of time, with the remainder going to the charity. Not only can you claim a tax deduction, but you may pay nothing on any capital gains from that asset. This is a really nice tool if you are charitably inclined, have a large capital gains situation, and have around $250,000 or more to place in the CRT.

- **Bunching** multiple years' worth of itemized deductions into a single year can help put you over the standard deduction threshold, allowing for itemized deductions that could then reduce your taxable income. This is a great option for any deductible expenses that you can time strategically, such as qualified medical expenses, charitable donations, or even paying state and local taxes. For instance, maybe you want to schedule two big medical procedures in the same year.

- **Harvesting capital gains and losses** is another strategy to reduce your tax burden. In the case of gains, if your income is low enough in a given year, you might qualify for a 0% tax rate for any long-term capital gains from selling investments that year. For example, in 2025, capital gains were taxed at 0% for single filers with a taxable income of $48,350 or less and for married filing jointly filers with a taxable income of $96,700 or less. When it comes to losses, selling investments at a loss can be used to offset other capital gains and up to $3,000 of ordinary income annually. If you still like the investment, you can always reinvest after 30 days (to avoid the wash rule that disallows the loss).

- **Investing in municipal bonds** or municipal bond funds can generate income that is often exempt from federal taxes and sometimes state taxes, making them an attractive investment for retirees in higher tax brackets (but see question 40 about the downside of municipal bonds).

- **Partial conversion to Roth IRAs** can be a good strategy if you're in a low tax bracket (for example, 12%), since systematically converting portions of a traditional IRA to a Roth IRA locks those dollars being taxed into a low bracket. This can also lower future RMDs.

- **Income from selling your home is tax-free** if you've lived in your home for at least two of the five years before selling. In recent years, any capital gains of up to $250,000 (or $500,000 for married couples filing jointly) have qualified as tax-free. This can be a significant tax-saving strategy for retirees looking to downsize.

- **Contributions to a 529 plan** for a grandchild's future education may not be deductible on your federal taxes, but the earnings grow tax-free, and withdrawals for qualified education expenses are also tax-free. Plus, some states offer tax deductions or credits for contributions.
- **Renting out your home, whether it's all or just part,** for fewer than 15 days a year can generate income that is tax-free.
- Certain types of **cash value life insurance** policies offer tax-free income through cash surrenders and then loans taken against the policy's cash value. This strategy requires careful planning to avoid inadvertently causing the policy to lapse. At death, any loans are paid off with tax-free death benefits.

I could write an entire book on these and other tax strategies for retirees. In fact, I have written one but never published it. Why? Because the world of tax strategies is constantly changing. What works this year may not work next year. So, to optimize your own tax situation, you'll either need to study each year's tax law changes (fun times!) or turn to an advisor such as a CPA who specializes in taxes or a CFP® who specializes in retirement issues. And by having read this chapter, you are now armed with the knowledge to ask them some good questions.

I could write an entire book on these and other tax strategies for retirees.

* * *

As they say, nothing is certain except for death and taxes. But that doesn't mean that specific tax rules will remain certain. The U.S. tax code is complicated (as the questions above illustrate), and you never know when and to what degree it will change. Every so often, new legislation will create significant tax implications for retirees. Consider the example of 2025's "One Big Beautiful Bill," which included a new deduction for people age 65 and older, depending on income, but that expires after four years. Kinda makes retirement tax planning a challenge.[24]

While wrapping one's head around tax rules isn't exactly anyone's idea of a fun retirement hobby, adapting to the rules and crafting smart tax strategies can still put hundreds of extra dollars in your pocket every single month. Even though you'll likely pay less in taxes than during your working years (goodbye, FICA!), you still need to stay on top of tax implications around Social Security benefits, pensions, IRAs, 401(k)s, and other income sources. The tax landscape is littered with costly land mines: Missing an RMD could cost you a brutal 25% penalty, taking the wrong kind of rollover could trigger unnecessary withholding, and even earnings from "tax-free" municipal bonds can end up increasing your Social Security taxes.

But armed with Randy's Rules of Tax Decisions and a solid understanding of strategies such as charitable giving, tax loss harvesting, and Roth conversions, you can keep more of your hard-earned money working for you instead of Uncle Sam. Remember, it's not about avoiding taxes altogether—it's about paying your fair share at the right time and in the most efficient way possible.

Now that we've covered how to keep more of your money in your own pocket through smart tax strategies, let's talk about how to keep it from slipping out the door undetected.

---

24 Working with a qualified financial advisor is a good way to keep abreast of the latest tax regulations. Or see my website (https://randylthurman.com/blog/) for articles on changes to tax rules and more. You can also visit the IRS Newsroom at https://www.irs.gov/newsroom for details on new and recent legislation affecting federal taxes.

Chapter 9

Threats and Hazards

"I've won a sweepstakes!" The voice on the other end of the phone was my client Steve. He had recently had some major health issues, needing a surgery that his insurance wouldn't cover, and he and his wife were in desperate need of money.

"That's exciting!" I answered.

"Yes, it's an answer to our prayers. And we don't even remember entering the contest!"

The hair on the back of my neck stood up. "Oh? Then how could you have won?"

"A man from the sweepstakes board called and told us. It's $200,000! Just what we needed for the surgery." Steve's wife, Jenny, added, "All we need to do to collect is pay a $1,200 administrative fee and provide our banking information. Then they'll immediately wire us the money! We were just about to call back the sweepstakes guy with our banking information but thought we should share the good news with you first."

I could feel their excitement through the phone, so I was dreading the warning I had to give them. "I really hate to break it to you, but this sounds like a scam. Sweepstakes winners almost always remember entering, they don't have to pay a fee to obtain their winnings, and they usually receive a check and not a wire transfer. Why don't you let me call for you to find out if it's legitimate?"

Steve was not happy with me. "I think you're wrong, but I'll bow to your judgment. His name is James, and here's his number, starting with country code first ..."

"Really? Country code?" I thought to myself. At least the code was for the United Kingdom, which is not a country known for phone scams. I called the number, and sure enough, good ol' James answered. I explained that I was a CPA helping my client who had just won his sweepstakes. I asked James, "And what sweepstakes did they enter?" He told me he'd have to "look it up," and there was a long pause.

Come to find out, my clients had supposedly won a Publishers Clearing House sweepstakes. When I pointed out that Publishers Clearing House was based in New York, not the UK, James was quick to share that he was part of the international disbursement division. *Oh, really?* I thought. He then added that he was thankful he could be the answer to their prayers. All he needed from me was their bank routing number, their account number, and their $1,200 fee to cover administrative expenses. Then, he would wire them their money within two days.

I asked him some questions: "Why is there a $1,200 fee?" His answer: "To cover administrative expenses." My next question: "Can you send us a check instead of wiring to reduce expenses?" James: "No." Me: "Can I get a physical address and then mail you the fee?" Him: "No." You get the drift. It was obviously a scam. Steve and his wife were brokenhearted when I let them know. But the outcome could have been worse—much worse.

It's vital for you to know about and prepare for the various threats and hazards you may face in your retirement years. Forewarned is forearmed. It's not just scams but other common financial threats as well. The information in this chapter won't make you any money, but it may keep you from losing it.

Question 43: How can I protect my retirement savings from an unexpected emergency?

"Things" happen: Your car gets stolen and your insurance won't pay to replace it; you get hit with a huge special assessment by your homeowners' association; you discover you've been hosting a colony of termites who've been dining on your house's foundation; a major health issue crops up and all the diagnostic testing will leave you on the hook for a huge hospital bill; you need to bail one of your kids out of jail; and the list goes on.

I've seen too many people who think, "Those sorts of things never happen to me." They fail to plan for the unexpected emergencies that happen to nearly everyone—and that take an unexpected chunk out of their retirement nest eggs.

I've seen too many people who think, "Those sorts of things never happen to me."

To be ready for a financial emergency, every good retirement plan needs to include a source of quick cash, or what's typically called a *cash reserve*. By cash, I mean money you can get to quickly with little to no loss when you need it. Here are some examples of cash reserve vehicles:

Every good retirement plan needs to include a source of quick cash.

- **Savings account.** The good ol' reliable. It doesn't offer much in terms of interest, but it provides easy access to your money and is insured by the FDIC up to $250,000.
- **Money market mutual fund.** The "grown-up" version of a savings account, it offers slightly higher interest rates. These funds are low-risk and while not FDIC insured, they're still considered relatively safe.
- **Short-term CD.** You're loaning money to the bank for a predetermined period, and in return, you get a fixed interest rate that's usually higher than a savings account or money market fund. The catch? You can't touch the money during that period without incurring a penalty. Generally, the shorter the time frame, the smaller the penalty. I recommend a one-year maturity and laddering multiple CDs so one will mature every three months. That way, you won't have to cash out the whole amount in case of emergency.
- **Treasury bills.** You're lending your money to Uncle Sam here. It's like going on a camping trip with the most dependable guy you know. These short-term securities are backed by the US government and, hence, considered to be one of the safest investments.
- **High-yield savings account or online savings account.** The digital age's gift to cash reserve investments. Typically, these offer higher interest rates than traditional savings accounts. Beware though: There are many scams in this area.

So, how much should you have in these types of accounts? The rule of thumb that most advisors agree on is three to six months of your monthly expenses plus any lump sum expenditure you expect over the next two years. Example: Your monthly expenditures are $5,000, and you plan on needing $25,000 for a new car (after trade-in) in about a year. On the low side, that calculates out to $40,000 in cash reserves (3 months × $5,000 + $25,000) and on the high side, to $55,000 (6 months × $5,000 + $25,000).

Beyond that amount, the rest of your retirement savings should be put to work. But even then, you don't want it all locked up in illiquid investments or investments that have, for example, a 7% surrender charge. Your savings should be invested where you can get to them quickly (say, five business days) and without big penalties.

Also remember that your cash reserve isn't invested to make your money grow. It's there for emergencies in which you need the money immediately. When you unexpectedly hit that hazard and you need cash quickly, it can become a major threat to your comfortable retirement not to have those funds readily available.

Your cash reserve isn't invested to make your money grow. It's there for emergencies.

Question 44: What are the biggest planning pitfalls that could threaten my retirement?

Let's talk about some of the big planning no-no's (that's another of my "technical" terms) that can trip you up on your way to finally settling down to read that pile of favorite books awaiting you by the fireside. You've heard about a few of these earlier in my discussion about financial storms (see chapter 7), but they bear repeating.

1. **Underestimating how long you'll live (i.e., longevity risk).** Living longer than you thought you would can be awesome, but having to go back to work at age 90 to pay the bills is probably not your idea of a comfortable retirement.

2. **Not accounting for inflation**, the sneaky little bugger that it is (i.e., inflation risk). If you're not planning for the price of everything to go up, you might be able to afford a nice restaurant dinner now, but in 20 years, you could find yourself living on a diet of ramen noodles.

3. **Making the wrong types of investments**—for example, any investment offering a big return with hardly any risk. Remember, if it sounds too good to be true … Also watch out for hazardous back-loaded investments in which you can't get your money out or have to pay a heavy surrender charge (I've seen penalties as large as 20%!) to do so. Now is not the time for illiquid investments. Putting all your eggs in one basket is also never a good idea unless it's a really, really sturdy basket, and even then, diversify! You don't want to reach retirement age to find your one basket has a hole in it, leaving you with too little to retire on. And don't get me started on trying to time the market! That's like trying to catch a falling knife: a potentially painful and fruitless endeavor.

In 20 years, you could find yourself living on a diet of ramen noodles.

4. **Not planning for healthcare costs.** This one is so big that I've devoted an entire explanation to it (see question 46).

5. **Forgetting about the downsides of debt.** Retiring with too much debt is like running a race with a weighted backpack. You may not make it to the finish line. It's better to shed those extra pounds before your retirement starting line so you can cruise into retirement without those interest payments weighing you down. While I generally don't

recommend taking money out of traditional IRAs or retirement plans to reduce debt because of their tax liabilities, if you have after-tax money you can use to pay off debt, I generally say go for it. Because when you're debt-free, you can better weather a lot of financial storms.

> **Retiring with too much debt is like running a race with a weighted backpack.**

6. **Oh boy, the tax "surprises"!** Not planning well for taxes can really bite you in the wallet. Taxes don't retire just because you do. For instance, withdrawals from certain retirement accounts can be fully taxable, and there can also be penalties for dipping in too early. On the flip side, you'll be penalized if you don't take enough out at certain ages. Having a long-term plan for income generation that's tax efficient will help you avoid these tax hazards.

7. **Failing to plan for the nonfinancial aspects of retirement.** Planning well isn't just about the money; it's also about what you're going to do with all your free time. I've seen people retire just to avoid the grind. They're not moving *toward* retirement; they're moving *away* from work. Not optimal. You need to have a purpose, a reason to get out of bed. Otherwise, retirement, from what I can tell, becomes a slow death. (A great book on the topic is *Purposeful Retirement* by Hyrum Smith. He's also one of the original

> **You need to have a purpose, a reason to get out of bed. Otherwise, retirement, from what I can tell, becomes a slow death.**

creators of the Franklin Day Planner and the author of another favorite book, *What Matters Most*.)

If you plan wisely and steer clear of these pitfalls, you're more likely to enjoy your golden years without dodging too many financial hazards. Remember, retirement is a phase of life that's supposed to be enjoyed, not spent worrying about the dangers ahead.

Question 45: Should I include illiquid investments in my retirement portfolio since I've heard they can generate a high return?

I consider most illiquid investments to be a hazard for retirees, since they don't allow you to get to your money when you might need it. (See question 43 for more on the importance of an emergency fund.)

By definition, an illiquid investment is one you cannot sell quickly. This type of investment typically lacks a ready market, and selling may take time, often due to difficulties in finding a ready and willing buyer. And for those illiquid investments that offer an option to get out quickly, this usually comes at a steep price due to hefty fees or penalties.

For instance, you may think that an investment in property in that up-and-coming part of town will only go up in value and net you a big gain. Or what about getting in on the ground floor of that promising start-up you heard about? Those might seem like great opportunities, but if you need to sell quickly, more often than not, you will take a beating. This could in turn threaten the health of your portfolio.

If you need to sell quickly, more often than not, you will take a beating.

My recommendation is generally to avoid illiquid investments for several reasons. Just like diversification, liquidity is important. Retirement really isn't a time to lock up your money. It will almost surely be a bad day when you find yourself needing cash and must sell an illiquid investment, if you can, to generate it. And mark my words, this will happen to nearly everybody—you included. Illiquid investments also often come with complex structures and risks that may be difficult to understand. Simple rule here: If you don't understand it, then steer clear (think cryptocurrency).

Here are some common types of illiquid investments that I typically discourage people from adding to their retirement portfolio:

- **Real estate.** Properties can be highly illiquid. Selling real estate often requires time for market listing, viewing, negotiation, and the closing process, which can take months or even years.
- **Back-end-loaded annuities.** Many annuity products have a hefty back-end sales charge for several years. This is what my dad labeled "get out fees." If you want to get out, he'd say, "It's going to cost ya." They generally will allow you to take 10% out annually without any charge, but after that, watch out! I've seen a surrender charge as high as 20% in the first ten years.
- **Long-term CDs.** Now, you wouldn't normally think of CDs as illiquid, but many of them have a hefty charge (you might even say penalty) if you cash in before their maturity date. The charge used to be about 12 months of interest for a five-year CD, but many times it's more. Personally, I don't like to go over 12 months on a CD for this reason (and some others). The extra interest is usually not

Personally, I don't like to go over 12 months on a CD.

worth the potential risk in the event you are locked in at a low rate when CD interest rates start rising.

- **Class B mutual fund shares.** These shares are often sold with the sales pitch that all of your money will be invested and you won't have to pay a sales load up front (as with class A shares). But you'll have higher internal expenses (which will impact your annual return), and if you cash them in, you'll pay what's called a *contingent deferred sales charge.* It can be as high as 8.5% but generally runs around 5% for five years or so. Only after that period will you be able to sell without incurring a charge.
- **Collectibles and art.** Yeah, I'm sure those Beanie Babies collectibles I bought in the late '80s are going to come back any day now. While unique and potentially of high value, items such as art, wine, or rare collectibles can be, I'll just say, very challenging to sell. The market for such items is niche, and finding the right buyer willing to pay the desired price can take time. Or never.

Despite all the pitfalls, I'm not saying you should never invest in illiquid investments. But if you're retired, then *almost* never. Yes, investing in illiquid assets can offer high returns and diversification benefits (for instance, those that move differently than the rest of your portfolio). If you're going to invest in any of these, it's important to approach with caution, ensuring they align with your overall investment strategy and liquidity needs.

Question 46: How should I plan for my healthcare costs?

Nobody can predict their future health, so medical costs can be a huge threat to retirement security—especially if you're retiring before Medicare kicks in at age 65. And even for those who retire at 65, a lot of people think that Medicare will cover everything. Spoiler alert: It doesn't. Here's a short list of what Medicare *doesn't* cover:

Medical costs can be a huge threat to retirement security—especially if you're retiring before Medicare kicks in.

- **Prescription drugs.** You can, however, purchase a separate Part D policy. Some Medicare Advantage plans also include prescription drugs.
- **Dental care.** Here, too, you can buy separate dental insurance, and some Medicare Advantage plans include this, albeit often with low annual limits.
- **Vision care.** Medicare generally doesn't pay for routine eye exams or glasses. Separate policies are available, and you can bundle vision and dental if you feel it's appropriate to your situation.
- **Hearing aids.** Medicare doesn't pay for routine hearing exams or hearing aids, but some Medicare Advantage plans do.
- **Medical costs outside the United States.** Traveling abroad? Medicare almost never covers care you receive outside the US, but most Medigap plans will cover up to 80% of the cost of emergency care abroad, up to a certain limit.

- **Deductibles and copayments.** With Medicare Part A, you're responsible for deductibles and copayments (in 2025, the deductible was $1,676). Long hospital stays will cost you some big bucks, too. Basically, Medicare covers 90 days and then 60 more days after that over your lifetime. At that point, it's all on you. With Part B, there's a $257 deductible and then a 20% copay beyond that amount.
- **Long-term care.** One of the largest potential expenses in retirement is the cost of long-term care. Medicare provides for some skilled nursing home services but nothing for custodial care. (More on this below.)

You can probably see the need to come up with a better plan than hoping Medicare will cover all your healthcare costs.

My recommendation? If you enroll in the original Medicare Part A and Part B coverages, then add a Medigap plan (also called *Medicare supplement insurance*) to help pay some of the out-of-pocket costs that Medicare doesn't cover. But beware: Medigap plans don't cover routine dental, hearing, or vision care. And make sure to buy a Medigap policy within six months of signing up for Medicare Part B. During that window, insurers can't reject you or charge more because of preexisting conditions.

Another option is a private Medicare Advantage plan, which is an alternative to original Medicare that typically includes the same coverages as Part A and Part B, plus Part D (prescription drugs) and other extra benefits such as dental, vision, and hearing. But if you have specific doctors or specialists you definitely want to see, then stay away from Medicare Advantage plans that require using their own provider networks.

One of the big financial hazards when it comes to healthcare is long-term care costs. The median annual cost of a private room in a nursing home was roughly $127,750 in 2024, and I can't imagine it's going anywhere but up.[25] Surprise! Medicare doesn't pay for long-term care for chronic illness or disability, and Medicaid will only kick in once your income and assets drop below a very low level.[26] The median stay in a nursing facility is five months.[27] However, the average stay for someone with Alzheimer's is two to three years.[28] So, it's important to consider a long-term care policy to protect yourself.

Surprise! Medicare doesn't pay for long-term care for chronic illness or disability.

But buying long-term care insurance is a darn tough decision. It can be very pricey, and benefits can vary widely. If you're self-insured (i.e., you have enough money to pay for long-term care yourself), lucky you. You probably don't need this insurance other than for peace of mind or to protect your other dollars. Otherwise, you'll need to take a hard look. The best time to buy long-term care insurance is usually before age 60 and when you're healthy. After 60, premiums become exorbitantly high. And if you already have health issues of almost any kind, more often than not, companies will tack on a hefty extra premium or deny you coverage. I suggest first shopping online without giving out your phone number. (Once they have your phone

25 "Calculate the Cost of Long-Term Care Near You," CareScout, https://www.carescout.com/cost-of-care.

26 Medicare will pay, after the copay, for a semiprivate, skilled nursing care facility for the first hundred days.

27 Anne Kelly et al., "Length of Stay for Older Adults Residing in Nursing Homes at the End of Life," *Journal of the American Geriatrics Society* 58, no. 9 (2010): 1702, https://doi.org/10.1111/j.1532-5415.2010.03005.x.

28 Ibid.

number, be ready for a steady stream of calls.) When you know the costs, then you can make an informed decision.

There's a lot more to consider and tons of books out there on making healthcare insurance decisions. I've read over a dozen. (See the resources section for my specific recommendations.)

Question 47: What are the most common scams you've seen that hit retirees so I can be prepared for them?

Unfortunately, retirees are victims of all types of financial scams (even though younger generations actually fall for scams more often). This could be because of retirees' perceived vulnerability, the fact that they usually have money, and the sad truth that their memory and cognition may not be as sharp as they once were.

There is a never-ending list of scams, and in almost four decades as an advisor, I have seen every one of these at least once.

- **Investment scams.** Scammers offer high returns on new products or opportunities that they say are once-in-a-lifetime chances. These often involve Ponzi schemes (does the name Bernie Madoff ring a bell?), pyramid schemes, or promises of quick and high returns with little to no risk. (See chapter 10 for a story about one of my clients who fell for a Ponzi scheme.) In the "pump and dump" investment scheme, as one example, telemarketers call seniors to tell them about a "wonderful" stock that's going to make them a lot of money, but "they must act now." What they are really doing is pushing a thinly traded stock owned by the brokerage company in order to create a buying frenzy. This artificially generates a lot of demand and a soaring stock price (the pump). Then, the brokerage company sells the stock (the dump) for a tidy profit and stops promoting it. This causes the stock price to plummet and erases any value for everyone else left holding shares.

- **Medicare/health insurance scams.** Scammers may pose as Medicare or insurance representatives to trick retirees into giving out sensitive personal financial information. Often, this is under the guise of saving money or getting them a rebate of premiums. As one example, just before the Medicare open enrollment period begins (around October 15), seniors may get a call from someone claiming to be from the Centers for Medicare and Medicaid Services, the agency that issues Medicare cards. To "verify" your identity, they will ask for your Social Security number and your bank routing and account numbers. These scammers can then use the information to commit identity theft. Just remember, like most government agencies and legitimate companies, Medicare will never call, email, or visit you to ask for your personal information.
- **Survivor and funeral scams.** Scammers trick mourning widows or widowers by claiming their deceased spouses owe them money. Or maybe they will say that they owe the deceased money and just need your banking info to send you the funds. Some unethical funeral homes may also try to overcharge families who are not familiar with funeral costs. I've been with clients and seen a funeral salesperson work the grieving family by saying, "It's the last thing you can do for them," then showing them the most expensive casket, services, etc.
- **Sweepstakes and lottery scams.** Scammers inform their targets that they have won a lottery or sweepstakes ("You must have forgotten you bought a ticket") and need to pay a small

amount to unlock the supposed prize. All the scammers ask for is a little banking information and/or a small fee. (Remember my clients Steve and Jenny?)

- **In-trouble-with-the-law scams.** Watch out for calls claiming that the police/sheriff/IRS agents are coming to your house right now to arrest you for unpaid tickets/back taxes/fines if you don't send money immediately to rectify the situation. "We can draft your account right now to keep you from being arrested," they offer as an alternative to keep you out of jail. It's a scary scam because the "sheriff" sounds real—and mad! Or maybe the caller says they are a grandchild or other close relative, pleading for help: "Grandma, it's Johnny. I'm in trouble and need bail money quick. Please talk to this police officer, and he'll tell you how you can send the money to get me out of jail." To make things worse, these scammers have begun using voice-cloning technology to mimic the actual voices of purported loved ones. According to the Federal Trade Commission, if you get one of these calls, it's best to hang up and call "Johnny" directly. Chances are, he's safe at home and has no idea what you're talking about.

> Scammers have begun using voice-cloning technology to mimic the actual voices of purported loved ones.

- **Romance scams.** Scammers create false profiles on dating sites or social media to strike up relationships and then trick people. The scammers start by building trust with their targets, sometimes posting or "chatting" several times a day. They continue to build that trust over time, even if there's always some excuse for why they can't meet in person or even over a video call. Eventually, they all need money for one reason or another, such as mom's new kidney surgery, money for plane tickets to travel to finally meet you, or you name it.

- **Internet fraud.** These types of scams could fill up a book. Here are the top ones I've seen:
    - *Phishing scams.* Phishing is a way that scammers trick you into giving them your personal information through fake emails, texts, or websites.
    - *Nigerian prince scam.* This scam, also known as an *advance-fee scam*, involves an email from a scammer claiming to be a foreign dignitary or someone wealthy who needs help moving money out of their country. They promise to share this wealth with you in exchange for an up-front payment.
    - *Fake tech support or billing scams.* The scammer pretends to be from a well-known tech company and tells you they've detected a problem, such as a virus, on your computer. Or maybe you receive a confirmation email for a subscription service that has been billed to your credit card even though you never subscribed. When you call the customer service agent to straighten things out, they offer to fix the problem but end up asking for a fee or even trying to gain access to your computer.

Unfortunately, these are only a few examples. Educate yourself and your loved ones about potential scams, and never give out personal information or money unless you're sure of the situation. Always keep your computer security up-to-date and be wary of any offers that seem too good to be true. (Have I said that before? Probably for a good reason.) Staying educated and vigilant is the best way to prevent becoming a victim of these scams.

I also recommend filling out a trusted contact form at financial institutions where you have your money. Banks can refer to this form in the unlikely event they suspect you are being scammed but can't talk you out of it. For example, you're certain Johnny needs the money to get out of jail. You're emotional and demand your bank send the money now. In that situation, the financial institution will call the trusted contact who can check it out or talk to you. "Oh, Johnny, he's here with me …"

I recommend filling out a trusted contact form at financial institutions where you have your money.

* * *

Chapter 9 exposed the less glamorous but absolutely crucial side of retirement planning—protecting yourself from the many threats and hazards that can derail your plans for your golden years. From Steve and Jenny's close call with the always too-good-to-be-true sweepstakes scam to the sneaky little bugger we call inflation, I've tried to clue you in to the financial booby traps that can catch even the savviest retirees off guard.

We explored protecting yourself with a solid cash reserve, avoiding the biggest planning pitfalls that trip up so many people, and taking a pass on no-go illiquid investments now that you're in retirement mode. We dove deep into the hazard of insufficient healthcare cost planning—because Medicare, despite what many people think, doesn't cover everything. Then there are the seemingly endless telephone and internet cons targeting retirees—from romance scams to fake tech support calls—with these rip-off artists getting increasingly creative and sophisticated in their approaches. The key takeaway? Being forewarned truly is being forearmed.

While the information in this chapter won't make you money, it can definitely help you keep the money you've worked so hard to accumulate. And here's some more good news: You don't have to navigate all these potential threats and financial hazards on your own—a great financial advisor can be your ally in both protecting your wealth and helping it grow. In the next chapter, I'll walk you through finding the right advisor for you.

Chapter 10

Do I Need a Financial Advisor?

"I'm changing advisors," Bill, a client of fifteen years, informed me one day.

"OK. You've been a client a long time. May I ask why?" I replied.

"Well, I know an advisor who's getting great returns—20% or more per year—with hardly any risk," he bluntly said. "He's doing a lot better than you, and he hasn't had a single down year."

I leaned in. "That's interesting. How's he doing that?"

Bill leaned back. "He has his system. He doesn't let people know what it is because then other people would steal it."

"You really need to check this guy out," I warned. "You know, if it sounds too good to be true …"

"I have checked him out," Bill retorted. "I've looked at some of his clients' statements and seen the big returns I've been missing out on because I've been investing with you. Besides, I trust him because he goes to my church." Bill was getting a little miffed at my questions. "Maybe you're just jealous," he added.

"Well, maybe I am," I responded, "but you owe it to yourself and your family to check out how this guy is getting better returns than anyone in the country without any down years."

Bill left and shortly after transferred his life savings to this new advisor. Not only that, but he also persuaded his dad to move his life savings over to this guy as well. I later learned that his new "advisor" was actually running a Ponzi scheme.[29] Bill and his dad both lost their entire savings.

Bill's sad story illustrates how important it is to do your due diligence. The advice in this chapter is no guarantee, but following it will go a long way toward eliminating any fraudulent advisors from getting a hold of your own hard-earned savings. For instance, the little things—such as asking potential advisors whether they have an independent, third-party custodian—can make a big difference.

A great advisor not only helps you with the analytical financial stuff but also gives you peace of mind. They can steer you away from making heat-of-the-moment decisions and help you refrain from making the "big emotional mistake" that a robo-advisor or go-it-alone management approach simply doesn't.

How do you find that great advisor? Read on.

Question 48: Should I hire a retirement advisor?

My short answer is yes. But I'll be the first to acknowledge that I'm biased on this question. After all, I'm a retirement advisor myself. That said, not everyone should hire one. If an advisor's benefits to you don't exceed their costs going forward, it's not worth hiring them.

---

29 For more on this case, see https://www.cftc.gov/PressRoom/PressReleases/5610-09.

So, how will you make that determination? I have an entire book on this topic (titled *Five Steps to Finding a Financial Advisor You Can Trust*) in case you'd like to dive deeper. In a nutshell, I recommend asking yourself two simple questions: What does it cost to hire a financial advisor? And do you have what it takes to manage your investments yourself?

What's the Cost?

It's generally not possible to determine the exact cost of hiring a financial advisor ahead of time, since there can be a huge range, often related to the dollar amount of your retirement portfolio. Advisors also calculate their fees in a number of different ways. But there are a few simple ways to estimate the cost.

The first thing to know is that some advisors are paid entirely from fees they charge their clients—that is, they are paid by you. Other advisors earn commissions from third parties each time they buy or sell an investment for you. I don't recommend commission-based advisors, since they may be more interested in selling you investment products that will earn them fat commission checks than in making sure your portfolio performs at its best.

I don't recommend commission-based advisors, since they may be more interested in selling you investment products.

Among fee-only advisors, some charge a flat fee, others an hourly rate, and still others a percentage of the value of the assets they manage for you. In the latter arrangement, the advisor is incentivized to grow the value as much as possible—which means your interests are aligned. And the percentage they charge typically drops according to how much money they are managing, since a fee of 1% on a very large portfolio will generate your advisor more money than 1.25% on a small portfolio.

As an example, if your retirement portfolio is $2 million, you might expect your advisor's fee to be around $20,000 (or 1%) per year.

At this point, you might be thinking to yourself, "Wow, that's a lot of money! Now that I'm retired, can I afford a retirement advisor? Is it really worth it to me?" The answer depends in part on how much value you place on expertise. Financial planning isn't easy. It takes many years of training and experience to get good at it—and to keep up with all the relevant changes to tax laws, market conditions, etc. (Remember all the complicated investment strategies from chapter 7 and all tax provisions from chapter 8?) Believe me, I've been doing it for decades, and I can tell you that financial planning takes a lot of work and is not easy to do well.

Which leads us to the second question you should ask yourself.

Do I Have What It Takes to Do It Myself?

In my experience, successfully managing one's own retirement portfolio requires three things: knowledge, time, and temperament.

By reading this book, you probably have a sense of the wide range of issues and the many details that will affect the financial success of your retirement plan. For instance, you'll need to develop a good grasp of the different types of investment vehicles, which strategies and techniques to apply to meet your particular goals, and all the various laws and regulations related to your situation. After all, it would be devastating if, after so many years of hard work and saving, your retirement dreams were to fall apart because you didn't know how to do the job right.

Successfully managing one's own retirement portfolio requires three things: knowledge, time, and temperament.

As with any skill, it also takes time to learn and then apply your knowledge. A surgeon once told me he could teach me the basics of performing an appendectomy in about three hours. Then he quickly added that I'd need to go through medical school and residency if I wanted to learn how to deal with the many unpredictable real-life situations I could face. I don't know about you, but I'd recommend you go with the surgeon over me for that job!

It's similar for financial planning. I'd say you should expect to read (and study) a minimum of ten books on investing—and I'm not talking about the how-to-beat-the-market-every-time, get-rich-quick-and-easy variety. (See the resources list for some excellent books I recommend for a serious education.)

You should expect to read (and study) a minimum of ten books on investing.

You should also have the time to take classes and maybe even gain some of the credentials required to become a qualified financial planner, such as CFP® certification. True, it takes about a thousand hours to complete that program, but it will give you the background you need in investing, taxes, retirement distributions, estate planning, and more. You should also plan to follow the ongoing changes and new developments in pertinent laws and regulations, not to mention what's going on in the investment markets. Of course, you'll also need to analyze and rebalance your own portfolio on a regular basis. In other words, expect to train for and to take on a new part-time job as your own retirement advisor.

This brings us to the final quality required to succeed—that is, temperament. Do you find yourself feeling interested in and energized by taking on this responsibility? Even more importantly, can you set aside your fears, worries, and even hopes when it comes to such an important job as managing your retirement portfolio yourself?

Studies have shown that the biggest factor in a person's long-term investment success is not their stock selection or timing the market. It's their behavior and emotions. When it comes to money, most people don't see things clearly. They're overconfident in their ability to predict the future and panic when the market drops and their investments lose value. The average investor doesn't have the emotional distance (not to mention the experience and training) to ride out the highs and lows and stick to a sound investment strategy. On top of that, results consistently indicate that retirement advisors outperform the "average investor" managing their own account by about 6%.[30] Just like performing surgery on a family member is usually not a good idea, the same could be said about managing your own money.

Retirement advisors outperform the "average investor" managing their own account by about 6%.

Let's face it—not everyone is cut out to manage their own retirement portfolio. If the above description doesn't fit you, maybe you're not one of those people. You'll do yourself an enormous favor by giving serious thought to hiring a trained professional to do the job for you. But if running spreadsheets and following the markets is your idea of a great way to spend your Saturday afternoon—and you can stay as cool as a cucumber as you watch the value of your life savings go up and down—then maybe it's time for you to put down this book and sign up for a CFP® course. That's more or less what I did.

30 Nick Murray, *Behavioral Investment Counseling* (The Nick Murray Company, Inc., 2008).

Question 49: What benefits will I gain from hiring an advisor?

Planning for retirement can feel like navigating a maze. There are so many decisions to make, from how to invest your savings to when to start taking Social Security, to name just two. The reality is that most people probably need some help not to get lost in the maze. This is where a retirement advisor can be a game-changer for you.

The reality is that most people probably need some help not to get lost in the maze.

Of course, the primary role of a retirement advisor is to help you meet your financial goal: to use your resources to maximize the probability you're going to be comfortable for the rest of your life (see question 27). Let me break down six specific reasons (not that there aren't more) why hiring one might be the smartest move you can make to achieve that goal.

1. **Coordinating tax strategies.** You don't stop paying taxes when you retire; in fact, managing them becomes even more crucial. (Remember all the questions in chapter 8 about taxes and the complex and ever-changing rules?) A retirement advisor will keep track of tax laws and help you create a tax-efficient strategy to ensure you keep more of your hard-earned money. They'll analyze your income sources—such as Social Security, pensions, and withdrawals from after-tax investment accounts and retirement accounts—to figure out the best way to minimize your taxes. I've seen situations in which good tax planning was what allowed someone to afford to retire comfortably.

2. **Crafting investment strategies.** Investing for retirement isn't as simple as choosing the right mutual fund or even picking stocks and bonds. It's about creating a strategy that aligns with your goals, risk tolerance, and time horizon. An advisor can help you properly diversify your portfolio, which means spreading out your investments in the right way to reduce risk and weather the storms. They'll also monitor the financial markets and rebalance your investments as needed to keep you on track. A good advisor will know that what might normally be a sound accumulation portfolio can be an awful retirement distribution portfolio.

3. **Deciphering Social Security benefits.** Social Security is a significant part of many people's retirement plans, but understanding when and how to claim benefits can be tricky. For example, if you start taking Social Security too early and are still earning over a certain amount of income, Uncle Sam will bite off a big chunk of your benefit. An advisor can guide you through this process, helping you decide the best time to start taking benefits. This decision can have a big impact on how much you receive over your lifetime, so it's essential to get it right.

4. **Navigating pensions, retirement plans, and IRAs.** Another significant part of most people's retirement income comes from pensions, retirement plans, and IRAs, and making decisions about these can also be tricky. For instance, with pension plans, an advisor will walk you through the pros and cons of taking a lump sum versus an annuity. This decision is irreversible and needs to be coordinated with your 401(k)s and IRAs. Penalties for messing up here can be as high as 25%.

5. **Evaluating cash flows.** It's vital to figure out how much money you'll need to live well in retirement. A retirement advisor can help you evaluate your expected cash flows by looking at your expenses, income, inflation, and any potential changes in your financial situation. They'll create a plan to ensure you have enough money to cover your needs without outliving your retirement funds. Just as importantly, they'll help you spend your money to live the retirement life you've planned. I've seen people who didn't plan right in their early years and ended up overspending. Now, they're struggling to get by, and it's too late to adjust their portfolios to do anything about it.

6. **Addressing other retirement issues.** Retirement advice isn't just about managing your finances; it's also about walking you through lifestyle changes and potential challenges, such as loss of a loved one, dealing with unexpected healthcare costs, or creating an estate plan. Many times, I've sat down with someone who has lost their spouse to reassure them that they're going to be OK financially and to help them figure out the changes to their Social Security income and their living expenses. A retirement advisor can help ensure that you have a comprehensive plan that covers all aspects of your retirement.

Retirement advice isn't just about managing your finances; it's also about walking you through lifestyle changes and potential challenges.

The Bottom Line

Hiring a retirement advisor can provide peace of mind and a well-structured plan for your future. They bring expertise and a personalized approach to your retirement planning, helping you navigate the complexities and make informed decisions. If you want to ensure a comfortable and secure retirement, partnering with a retirement advisor might be one of the best investments you can make. Even though I'm biased, I think my clients would back me up on that claim.

Question 50: How can I find a trustworthy retirement advisor?

Here are six fundamental questions you absolutely must ask before you set up an appointment to meet with a potential retirement advisor. (I go into a lot more detail in my book on this subject.) These questions should eliminate 90% of advisors and help you home in on the right one for you. Keep them in mind starting with your first visit to their website.

1. Is the advisor a fiduciary on all accounts, all of the time?

This question is numero uno—and a deal-breaker. But wait, you may be asking, "What is a fiduciary?" A fiduciary is a professional who is legally obligated to act in the best interests of their clients. This means they must put your needs and goals above their own financial interests. You would think that everyone who calls themselves a financial advisor would be a fiduciary. Maybe they *should* be, but that's not usually the case. Believe it or not, the overwhelming majority of financial advisors are *not* fiduciaries.

It is essential to work with a financial advisor who is a fiduciary, since their primary responsibility will be to help you make informed decisions about your financial future. Non-fiduciary advisors are not held to the same ethical standards, and their advice may be influenced by earning commissions or other financial incentives for themselves.

The answer to this question generally can be found on the advisor's website, since most fiduciaries want you to know that they are one. If they don't say so, they probably aren't a fiduciary. You can also ask them when you talk to them by phone. If you get to that "interview" stage, I would ask again if they are a fiduciary "on all accounts, all of the time." Sometimes they can act as a fiduciary on some accounts but not on others. If they don't respond with an emphatic "*Yes!*" then it's time to move on.

2. What certifications has the advisor earned?

Seek out only those professionals holding recognized financial certifications and degrees. These designations are intended to indicate excellence in their line of work. A financial advisor should have at least one of the following credentials (I have listed them in what I consider the order of importance for a retiree):

- CFP®—Certified Financial Planner®
- CPA/PFS™—Personal Financial Specialist™ (a certified public accountant who has a specialty in financial planning)
- ChFC®—Chartered Financial Consultant®
- CFA®—Chartered Financial Analyst®

The organizations that grant these designations require an advisor to pass an initial exam and obtain continuing professional education. By choosing a planner with one or more of these designations, you can be comfortable that the planner has made a commitment to excel in financial planning.

You can almost always find their certifications on their website, typically listed following their name. And if you are having trouble finding a CFP® in your area, take a look on the CFP® Let's Make a Plan[31] web page. (Some of the designations and the organizations that regulate them are listed in the glossary at the end of this book.)

3. How does the advisor get paid?

Generally, financial advisors are either commission-based, fee-based, or fee-only.

Commission-based advisors make money from commissions on selling you financial products. The more they sell, the better they do. I see many conflicts of interest here, and these types of advisors tend to keep quiet in terms of how much they get paid.

Fee-only advisors are paid by you, the client. They are free from outside financial influences. Theirs is a client-driven approach that eliminates many of the conflicts of interest otherwise found in the financial advisor world. These advisors tend to be transparent about their compensation. You know how much and by whom they are getting paid.

Fee-only advisors are paid by you, the client. They are free from outside financial influences.

Fee-based advisors earn a combination of commission and fees. They may charge you for a financial plan and then implement it by selling some of their commission-based products.

Understanding the three methods should help you make informed decisions.

31 https://www.letsmakeaplan.org/find-a-cfp-professional

So, look for the words *fee-only* on their website. If you can't find it, they probably aren't, since fee-only advisors typically want you to know this information. And if you're having trouble finding a fee-only advisor near you, take a look online at the Fee-Only Network[32] or The National Association of Personal Financial Advisors[33].

4. How many years of experience does the advisor have?

As a rule, if you have $100,000 or more in assets to invest, consider only planners who have experienced at least one market downturn *and* who have five or more years of experience. That's not to say there aren't some very good planners with fewer years in the business, but experience often counts. You probably don't want to hire an advisor who is cutting their financial advisory business teeth on your retirement nest egg.

For the next two questions, it's time for a phone call. You should get these answers before you set an appointment to meet.

5. What's their investment portfolio minimum?

Many financial advisors require a client to meet a minimum investment portfolio value in order to work with them. This minimum can vary significantly, with some advisors requiring as little as $5,000, while others may require $1 million or more. It is crucial to understand an advisor's minimum investment requirements. No need to waste anyone's time. If their minimum is too high for you, look for an advisor with a minimum that matches your situation.

32 https://www.feeonlynetwork.com/

33 https://www.napfa.org/find-an-advisor

6. Do they offer a free initial consultation?

Now that you've done your initial due diligence and know you can meet their minimum, you should ask this question before setting up an in-person meeting. Most advisors will offer a free initial consultation, so you want to hear a "Yes" here. An advisor should take the time to see if you are a good match for each other. Besides, it would seem odd to me if someone would ask you to pay them before they even know whether they can help you. If an advisor is oriented toward working with you over the long term, they should be willing to invest an hour to see if you are a good fit. It's a win-win in the long run.

There you have it. Asking these six questions will eliminate 90% of the advisors out there and save you a lot of time. Now you're ready for your initial consultation. (In question 52, I'll recommend some questions for you to ask then—and what you want to hear.)

Question 51: What are robo-advisors, and are they a good choice for me?

Real-life human financial advisors can be costly and often require a minimum investment. And if an advisor can't demonstrate value over time, then maybe they're not worth what you're paying them. On top of that, it's not always easy to find a good one in the first place. But for many people, managing their own retirement portfolio may also feel overwhelming, especially for someone who is new to it or doesn't have a lot of time to handle all their investments.

So, what's the alternative to an advisor or a do-it-yourself (DIY) approach? This is where robo-advisors come into play as a third option. First, what are robo-advisors, and how do they work? Let's dive in and see if they might be a good fit for you.

What's a Robo-Advisor?

Robo-advisor is a funny-sounding name to me. It reminds me of the 1987 sci-fi film *RoboCop*. *Robo-advisor* is actually the term for a computerized financial planner. I can picture some techno nerds saying to themselves, "You know, about 90% of this financial planning stuff could be computerized."

The first robo-advisors came out in 2008—remember the Great Recession?—and the initial versions were pretty basic and didn't really do much more than calculate future values, input a budget, and such. Since then, they've come a long way. Nowadays, to design an efficient retirement portfolio based on your risk tolerance and goals, you can just enter your data (although this can itself be a lengthy and exhaustive process), then hit the "calculate" button. Voila! In about 50 milliseconds, give or take, out pops your retirement plan.

Voila! In about 50 milliseconds, give or take, out pops your retirement plan.

Benefits of Using Robo-Advisors

So why might you want to use a robo-advisor instead of hiring a CFP®?

- **Lower fees.** The cost of using robo-advisors is much lower compared to traditional advisors, which is one of their biggest advantages. Traditional commission-based financial advisors may earn up to a 6% commission up front. Fee-only advisors like me typically charge around 1% of the assets under management per year and have minimums. But robo-advisors typically charge a fraction of that—often around 0.25% to 0.50% of assets under management. This lower cost can be a significant advantage, especially for a small investor whose portfolio's value falls below an advisor's minimum.

- **Accessibility.** Robo-advisors are accessible 24/7 to anyone with an internet connection, making investing more approachable for the average person. They're great if you have a question at 2 a.m. or during tax season, when it may be tough to get a quick answer from your CFP®.

But robo-advisors typically charge a fraction of that—often around 0.25% to 0.50% of assets under management.

- **Ease of use.** These platforms are user-friendly and can be set up with minimal effort and at any time. Want to set yours up on a Sunday afternoon or a weekday evening? No problem.
- **Automated rebalancing.** Robo-advisors automatically rebalance your portfolio to maintain your desired asset allocation, ensuring that your investments stay aligned with your goals. Most advisors also do this, but some do not (see "Other questions you should ask" below).

Problems with Robo-Advisors

While robo-advisors have many benefits, they are not without their drawbacks. Here are some potential issues to consider:

- **Limited personalization.** Robo-advisors use algorithms based on the information you provide, which might not capture your unique financial situation or needs. Their data sheets can't cover all areas, or they would be enormous. For example, what if you have tax loss carryforwards, previous marriages over ten years, a deceased previous spouse, a tax-deferred annuity from before 1986, special state rules for a 529 plan, etc.? There are nearly endless unique situations.

- **Lack of human interaction.** If you prefer speaking with a person for reassurance or detailed explanations, you will find robo-advisors lacking. What happens when you want to know why your last transaction triggered the wash rules and you didn't get to take the loss you thought you generated? A human simply does a better job answering questions like this. True, some robo-advisors offer a personal advisor service, but to put it bluntly, the ones I've seen are awful. They know nothing about taxation, estate planning issues, or sometimes even retirement portfolios.

> **If you prefer speaking with a person for reassurance or detailed explanations, you will find robo-advisors lacking.**

- **Behavioral finance aspects.** This, I've seen in the real world, is the biggest drawback, and there's been a lot of research backing it up. Investing success, to a very large degree, is about managing emotions. Say things are looking bad, the market is down, and you want to go to cash. You figure you'll get back in when you "feel better." When do you feel better? When the market's back up, of course. Turns out you sold low and bought high—a bad combination. Robo-advisors can't provide the emotional support or guidance of a human advisor, who can counsel you during those market downturns.

- **Complex financial needs.** If you have complex financial needs or require estate planning, tax advice, or retirement planning, a robo-advisor might not be able to fully address your requirements. Have a child with special needs? There are certain things you need to do that I've never seen a robo-advisor suggest. Have a spendthrift child or a child with an addiction? Again, there are certain things you need to do to protect them and your finances. Today's robo-advisors simply can't cover all the complexities.

Great Robo-Advisors to Consider for Retirees

Several robo-advisors have gained popularity because of their reliability and performance. Some of the top ones are listed below, with more details in the resources list at the end of this book:

- Betterment
- Wealthfront
- Vanguard Digital Advisor
- Schwab Intelligent Portfolios
- Boldin (formerly New Retirement)

Are Robo-Advisors a Good Choice for You?

Robo-advisors can be an excellent choice if the following are true:

- You are new to investing and need a straightforward, low-cost entry point.
- You prefer a hands-off, and lower-cost, approach to managing your investments and are knowledgeable in the area of retirement financial issues.
- You have relatively simple financial planning needs.
- You want automated portfolio management and rebalancing.

- You are emotionally secure and disciplined to stay the course with your investment plan, especially when things look bad.

Robo-advisors are *not* a good choice if the following are true:

- You have complex financial needs, including estate issues and complex tax strategies.
- You prefer personalized advice.
- You are like most human beings, who need emotional support during market downturns.
- You might benefit more from a traditional financial advisor.

Robo-advisors offer an innovative and cost-effective way to invest, making it easier for many people to access financial planning and investment management. But I see two major strikes against them. First, in my long experience with retirees, behaviors and emotions are generally their key stumbling blocks in achieving their goals, and no robo-advisor can really address that. Second, when it comes to managing the interworkings and complexities of investment, tax, and estate issues common to retirees, robo-advisors just don't seem to be there … at least not yet.

Question 52: What other questions should I ask a potential advisor?

The questions you've asked so far are a great start (see question 50). They will eliminate about 90% of the advisors out there. Here are the other questions I recommend you ask to find that top 2% advisor.

1. "In the unlikely event things don't work out, what are the costs to move my money out from your management?"

This is a big one. What you want to hear is "Nothing," or "The custodian charges $100 [that is, a nominal fee]" or something like that. Many times, I've seen back-end loads of around 5% to 7%, sometimes as high as 20%! Crazy stuff. With a fee-only advisor, you don't have to worry about those sorts of fees. But if an advisor is commission- or fee-based, you need to know.

2. "How often will we meet?"

What you *don't* want to hear is, "Everything is so well set up, we won't have to meet at all." Instead, you *do* want to hear something like, "Initially, we will meet quarterly (or semiannually). Eventually, we will meet on an annual basis or more often as needed."

3. "What is the portfolio you are recommending to me and why?"

Here, you want to understand why the advisor is making a particular recommendation. How is it tailored to your needs? What are the expectations for negative years (since they will come)? How great can the good years be and how bad can the bad years be for any one-, five-, and ten-year time frame and within what level of confidence (they should answer 95% or higher)?

4. "What are the tax strategies you would apply in my situation?"

What you *don't* want to hear is something like, "We aren't CPAs, so we don't give tax strategies." You *do* want to hear the advisor mention things such as tax loss harvesting, tax-efficient funds, tax-free bonds, and retirement plans.

5. "How often will you rebalance my portfolio?"

Expect to hear something like, "We evaluate rebalancing on a quarterly basis. If your portfolio needs rebalancing, we do so." What you *don't* want to hear is, "We don't rebalance."

What you *don't* want to hear is something like, "We aren't CPAs, so we don't give tax strategies."

6. "What are the RMD rules?"

This is more of an "Are they *really* a retirement advisor?" question. They should be able to tell you the age at which you must start taking a distribution, an approximate percentage, the penalty for missing a distribution, all about qualified charitable distributions, etc. What you don't want to hear is something like, "I'm not really sure what that is, but I can look it up."

7. "How often will I receive statements, and do I have online access to my account?"

You should hear, "At least quarterly" and "Yes." Nothing less is acceptable.

8. "If I need to take money out in a hurry, how long will it take?"

A normal response is five business days or less. If you hear something like "A couple of months" or longer, move on.

9. "How often will I receive performance reports?"

Performance reports show you how your portfolio is doing and how well you are meeting your objectives. If you are investing more money or withdrawing funds, it's really tough to track this on your own. You should expect to receive a performance report quarterly. Annually is a little too long, and "We don't do performance reports" is totally unacceptable.

10. "Will I receive a tax letter at the end of the year detailing everything my tax preparer needs to know about my investment account?"

Tax laws are complex. You'll need to know the nature of your gains. Are they long- or short-term? You'll also need to know if you earned qualified dividends or tax-free interest. All these details and amounts should be spelled out for the most analytic tax preparer. In other words, you want to hear a "Yes" here. You'll also want to know when you will receive your tax letter. Many come a little bit later than regular 1099 forms (that is, late February), but your tax letter should arrive no later than the end of February.

11. "What are the costs, including taxes, for me to move my portfolio over to you?"

Sometimes, moving money can result in what's called *unrealized gains*. If you sell and move your money over to a new advisor, you may trigger capital gains tax on these gains. Sometimes, your current advisor may also charge big fees to move your money to a new advisor. Find out before you move.

12. "If you were me, what questions would you ask that I haven't?"

This is my go-to final question. You never know what you might have missed, but a good advisor should be able to tell you.

Finding a retirement advisor you can trust takes some time on the front end in order to ask the right questions. Based on my knowledge of the industry, I've shared the questions I would ask if I were in your shoes—questions that a lot of advisors probably wish you wouldn't bring up. While no method is perfect, I designed this process to help you find a top 2% financial advisor for your retirement and weed out the others.

I designed this process to help you find a top 2% financial advisor.

* * *

So, do you need a financial advisor? Asking me this question is a bit like asking a barber, "Do I need a haircut?" I'll always consider working with a financial advisor to be a good decision. Perhaps the real question isn't whether engaging an advisor is worth it to you but whether *you* have what it takes to go it alone. Successfully managing your own retirement portfolio requires the trifecta of knowledge, time, and temperament—and in my experience, most people are missing at least one of these ingredients. Think of it this way: Would you perform surgery on yourself after watching a few tutorials on YouTube? If not, why trust your hard-earned life savings to an amateur money manager like yourself?

So, to help you find the right professional to help you, this chapter has summarized my ultimate guide to advisor shopping, complete with six must-ask questions to eliminate 90% of the pretenders (starting with the big one: "Are you a fiduciary?"). Regarding robo-advisors, or what you might consider a middle ground between DIY disaster and real-life human hand-holding, keep in mind that algorithms can't talk you off the ledge when the market crashes and you're tempted to sell everything and stuff your mattress with cash.

In the end, I've left you with a twelve-question arsenal that should identify—and impress—the most seasoned advisor for you. After all, you deserve to find someone you can trust to help make your retirement dreams come true.

Conclusion

As we've explored throughout these 52 questions, understanding retirement finances encompasses far more than simply determining how much money to withdraw each month from your 401(k). Crafting a solid retirement plan is a multifaceted journey that touches every aspect of your life—from emotional readiness to investment strategies, from tax planning to protection against financial hazards. By addressing these questions thoughtfully and proactively, you've taken a big step toward securing the retirement you deserve.

I'm reminded of my client Margaret, a brilliant engineer who had meticulously saved for 30 years. When we first met, she confidently announced she had retirement "all figured out." Yet, as we worked through these questions together, her eyes widened with each new consideration. "I had no idea there were so many moving parts," she confessed during our third meeting. "I was focused entirely on hitting my savings number but hadn't thought about tax strategies, healthcare planning, or how to actually create income from my nest egg." Today, Margaret enjoys a fulfilling retirement teaching part-time at a local college while traveling extensively—all because she took the time to address these questions before making the leap. Like Margaret, you now have the tools to transform uncertainty into confidence.

And remember, retirement planning isn't a one-time event but an ongoing process. Life brings changes, markets fluctuate, and laws evolve. Revisit these questions periodically, especially during major life transitions. Whether you choose to navigate this journey independently or with professional guidance (which I highly recommend), the knowledge you've gained here will serve as your compass, keeping you on track to your destination. Your retirement years represent one of life's great adventures. Navigate them with the same care, curiosity, and confidence that you've demonstrated by engaging with this book.

Here's to your worry-free retirement journey!

Resources

Look, I get it. You're probably drowning in retirement advice right now, including everything you just heard from me in this book! Every time you turn around, another "expert" wants you to buy their book or attend their seminar, promising to unlock the secret to your perfect retirement. But here's the thing—after decades of working with clients just like you, I've learned that these one-size-fits-all programs aren't for most retirees. Your retirement plan will be as unique as you are, incorporating a wide range of advice (and not just mine). That's why I'm sharing with you this list of websites and books to help you put together the pieces that fit for you.

To create this list, I didn't just Google "best retirement books" and call it a day. I have personally vetted every single item listed below. These are the resources I actually use, recommend to my own clients, and sometimes even gift to family members. Each one has helped real people navigate real retirement challenges without the fluff or false promises you'll find elsewhere.

Picture me sitting across the table from you over a cup of coffee, sharing the tools that I know will genuinely make a difference for you. Consider them your tool kit for transforming retirement anxiety into retirement confidence as this new stage of life finally arrives.

Life Expectancy and Inflation Planning

Actuaries Longevity Illustrator

https://www.longevityillustrator.org/

A good site to learn more about the difference between longevity and life expectancy.

Healthy Life Expectancy Calculator

https://apps.goldensoncenter.uconn.edu/HLEC/

Complete a short questionnaire. I like this one because it predicts the longest life for me!

Living to 100

https://www.livingto100.com/

This longer questionnaire also generates suggestions for adding years to your life.

Life Expectancy Calculator

https://lifeexpectancycalculator.com/

Answer about twenty short questions and get immediate results by email.

R-CPI-E (CPI for Americans aged 62 and older)

https://www.bls.gov/cpi/research-series/r-cpi-e-home.htm

This index includes the basket of goods most closely resembling the actual spending patterns of people aged 62 and up—and it's the index I recommend that retirees use for planning purposes.

Medicare/Healthcare

HealthCare.gov: Health Coverage for Retirees

https://www.healthcare.gov/retirees/

This government website explains different options for health coverage, including for people who retire before age 65 and don't have a retiree health plan.

10 Costly Medicare Mistakes You Can't Afford to Make
by Danielle Kunkle Roberts

This book exposes common Medicare pitfalls and how to avoid them. It draws from the author's extensive industry experience to help readers prevent penalties and make informed decisions.

It's Not That Complicated
by Ari Parker

This book breaks down Medicare into three key decisions through accessible metaphors and straightforward language (comparing Medicare choices to ordering pizza) to help readers understand their options.

Prepare for Medicare: The Insider's Guide to Buying Medicare Insurance
by Matt Feret

This book provides candid answers to pressing Medicare questions from the perspective of a 20-year industry veteran, helping readers choose appropriate plans while avoiding marketing traps. The companion *Prepare for Medicare Workbook* serves as a practical tool with interactive exercises and planning guides that allow readers to organize their Medicare information and work through the decision-making process step by step.

Social Security

The Social Security Administration website has a wealth of information. Here are a few particular pages worth checking out.

Social Security Administration
https://ssa.gov

Plan for Retirement estimator
https://www.ssa.gov/prepare/plan-retirement

Frequently asked questions
https://www.ssa.gov/faqs/en/

Social Security–related scams
https://www.ssa.gov/scam

Social Security Quick Calculator
https://www.ssa.gov/oact/quickcalc/index.html

Reverse Mortgages

While I don't recommend a reverse mortgage for most people, if you're considering the option, it's critical to understand all the details. You can read more on these websites.

Home Equity Conversion Mortgages for Seniors
https://www.hud.gov/program_offices/housing/sfh/hecm/hecmhome

Reverse Mortgage Daily
https://www.housingwire.com/reverse-mortgage/

What Is a Reverse Mortgage?
https://www.consumerfinance.gov/ask-cfpb/what-is-a-reverse-mortgage-en-224/

Investment Analysis Tools

Morningstar Investor

https://www.morningstar.com/mm/investor/portfolio-management-tools

This tool provides in-depth research, analyst reports, and a unique "Portfolio X-Ray" feature for detailed analysis of asset allocation, sector weightings, and fees. Monthly fee (billed annually).

Ziggma

https://ziggma.com

Provides professional-grade portfolio analysis at a reasonable price, including portfolio scoring, unlimited account connections, and risk assessment tools. Free version available.

Portfolio Visualizer

https://www.portfoliovisualizer.com

Offers advanced tools such as backtesting, Monte Carlo simulations, and factor analysis to help investors test and refine their strategies. Free tier available.

Retirement Planning Tools

Betterment

https://www.betterment.com

Often seen as the pioneer in robo-advisors. Known for its ease of use and comprehensive financial planning tools. Charges 0.25% per year of the amount under management.

Boldin (formerly New Retirement)
https://www.boldin.com
A relatively new retirement planner and robo-advisor. You can try a much-watered-down version for free, but the real value is the Planner Plus paid version.

Schwab Intelligent Portfolios
https://www.schwab.com/intelligent-portfolios
No advisory fees, but you need to have a minimum investment amount of $5,000.

Vanguard Digital Advisor
https://investor.vanguard.com/advice/robo-advisor
Backed by the reputable Vanguard brand, this tool combines low costs with strong investment strategies. No cost for the first 90 days; after that, 0.20%.

Wealthfront
https://www.wealthfront.com
Like Betterment, this tool has low fees and a lot of customization options. Offers a wide range of services, including tax loss harvesting. Charges 0.25% a year.

Investing Strategies

Asset Allocation: Balancing Financial Risk
by Roger Gibson
A comprehensive guide to diversification strategies that explains why asset allocation is crucial for managing risk while generating returns in retirement portfolios.

The All-Weather Retirement Portfolio
by Randy L. Thurman
Presents a balanced investment approach designed to perform well across various economic conditions, helping retirees maintain financial stability regardless of market environments.

Investment Policy: How to Win the Loser's Game
by Charles Ellis
Explains why trying to beat the market is counterproductive and offers a disciplined investment policy framework for retirees focused on long-term success rather than short-term speculation.

The Bogleheads' Guide to Retirement Planning
by Taylor Larimore et al.
A practical, straightforward guide based on John Bogle's low-cost investing principles, covering everything from asset allocation to tax efficiency for retirement investors.

The Intelligent Investor
by Benjamin Graham
Warren Buffett's mentor provides timeless wisdom on value investing, emphasizing the importance of patience, discipline, and emotional control—particularly valuable lessons for retirees.

The Prudent Investor's Guide to Beating Wall Street at Its Own Game
by John Bowen
Outlines strategic approaches for retirees to achieve consistent returns while minimizing risks through prudent investment decisions and institutional-level portfolio management.

The Four Pillars of Investing
by William Bernstein
Explores the four fundamental elements of successful investing: theory, history, psychology, and business, providing retirees with a comprehensive framework for making informed decisions.

The Elements of Investing
by Burton Malkiel and Charles Ellis
A concise, accessible primer on investing fundamentals that distills complex concepts into straightforward principles, perfect for retirees seeking clarity in their financial decisions.

The Investment Answer Book
by Daniel C. Goldie
A clear road map through the overwhelming world of personal finance that breaks down the investment process into five essential decisions and empowers readers to build confidence while avoiding costly mistakes.

Behavioral Finance and Money Psychology

Purposeful Retirement and What Matters Most
by Hyrum Smith
Purposeful Retirement is a great book on understanding your purpose in retirement. Hyrum Smith is also one of the original creators of the Franklin Day Planner and the author of another favorite book, *What Matters Most.*

The Psychology of Money
by Morgan Housel
A thoughtful collection of stories exploring how people think about money, showing that successful financial decisions stem more from behavior than intelligence and highlighting how personal history, worldview, and ego shape our relationship with money.

Happy Money: The Science of Happier Spending
by Elizabeth Dunn and Michael Norton
Based on innovative research, this book reveals that the secret to getting more happiness from your money isn't necessarily having more but spending it differently, with practical guidelines for making purchasing decisions that maximize happiness.

Why Smart People Make Big Money Mistakes—and How to Correct Them
by Gary Belsky and Thomas Gilovich
Examines the psychological traps that lead even intelligent people to make costly financial errors, offering clear explanations of cognitive biases such as loss aversion and mental accounting along with practical strategies to overcome them.

Behavioral Finance: Understanding the Social, Cognitive, and Economic Debates
by Edwin Burton and Sunit Shah
A comprehensive examination of how psychology influences financial decisions, explaining why investors often act irrationally and how awareness of these behavioral patterns can lead to better retirement planning outcomes.

Nudge: Improving Decisions About Health, Wealth, and Happiness
by Richard H. Thaler and Cass R. Sunstein
Explores how subtle changes in how choices are presented can significantly impact financial decision-making, with valuable insights for retirees on structuring their financial environment to promote better outcomes.

Predictably Irrational: The Hidden Forces That Shape Our Decisions
by Dan Ariely
Reveals the predictable patterns behind seemingly irrational financial behaviors, helping retirees understand and counteract the psychological forces that can lead to poor money management in retirement.

Thinking, Fast and Slow
by Daniel Kahneman
Written by the Nobel Prize–winning psychologist, this book explains the two systems that drive how we think—the fast, intuitive system and the slow, deliberative system—and how they affect our financial decisions, particularly crucial for retirees.

Your Money and Your Brain
by Jason Zweig
Examines the neuroscience behind financial decisions, explaining why our brains often lead us to counterproductive investment behaviors and offering practical strategies for retirees to make more rational financial choices.

Glossary

401(k)
A retirement savings plan sponsored by an employer that allows employees to save and invest a portion of their paycheck before taxes are taken out. Taxes are paid upon withdrawal, as defined in IRS Code section 401(k). Also available as a Roth 401(k).

403(b)
A retirement plan like a 401(k) but designed for employees of public schools and certain nonprofit organizations, as defined in IRS Code section 403(b). Also available as a Roth 403(b).

457 plan
A type of nonqualified, tax-advantaged deferred-compensation retirement plan available primarily for governmental employees, as defined in IRS Code section 457.

1099 form
This IRS form reports various types of income other than wages, salaries, and tips. There are several types, such as the 1099-INT for interest income or the 1099-MISC for miscellaneous income.

Adjusted gross income (AGI)

This is your total gross income minus specific deductions, such as student loan interest or contributions to retirement accounts. It's a key number because it determines your eligibility for many deductions and credits.

Annual earnings test

This is a test to determine how much of your Social Security benefits may be reduced if you work and receive benefits before reaching full retirement age. If you earn over a certain limit, your benefits will be temporarily reduced.

Asset allocation

This is the strategy of dividing your investment portfolio among different asset categories, such as stocks and bonds. It also includes dividing your stocks into large cap and small cap, US and international, growth and value, etc. The goal is to balance risk and reward based on your investment goals, risk tolerance, and time horizon.

Average monthly earnings (AME)

Your AME is calculated based on your highest 35 earning years (computational years) divided by the number of months. This average is used to determine the amount of your Social Security benefits.

Blue chip stock

Blue chip stocks are shares in large, reputable, and financially sound companies with a history of reliable performance. They are often considered safer investments than, say, aggressive growth stocks. (See also *large cap*, *mid cap*, *small cap*, *emerging market*, *growth*, *international*, and *value stock*.)

Bond

Bonds are loans to governments or companies. In return, bond buyers receive regular interest payments and the return of their original investment when the bond matures. They are generally considered safer than stocks but usually offer lower returns. (See also *high-yield bond*, *I bond*, *municipal bond*.)

Business risk

This is the risk that a company will perform poorly, leading to a decline in the value of its stocks or bonds. Factors such as poor management, strong competition, or economic downturns can increase business risk. (See also *inflation risk*, *interest rate risk*, *market risk*.)

Capital gain

Capital gains are the profits from the sale of an asset such as stocks or real estate. If you sell for more than you paid, the difference is your capital gain. This gain is subject to different tax rates depending on how long you held the asset.

Cash reserves

Funds that are set aside, in a very liquid account, to be used in times of financial difficulty or emergency. The general rule of thumb is to reserve an amount equal to three to six months of living expenses.

Catch-up provision

A tax-advantaged feature of some retirement savings plans that allows individuals aged 50 or over to make additional contributions beyond the regular contribution limits. This helps older workers save more as they approach retirement. This applies to IRAs and any contributory plans, including 401(k), 403(b), and 457.

Certificate of deposit (CD)

CDs are savings products offered by banks with fixed interest rates and fixed terms. They are considered very safe but usually offer lower returns than other investments.

Certified Financial Planner® (CFP®)
A professional designation for financial planners, awarded by the Certified Financial Planner® Board of Standards, Inc. to individuals who meet stringent education, examination, experience, and ethics requirements.

Certified public accountant (CPA)
A designation given to licensed accounting professionals by a state board of accountancy. They must pass a rigorous exam and adhere to continuing education requirements. CPAs are qualified to handle a variety of accounting and tax-related tasks.

Certified Public Accountant/Personal Financial Specialist™ (CPA/PFS™)
A credential for CPAs who specialize in personal financial planning. They have demonstrated expertise in areas such as tax planning, estate planning, retirement planning, and investment strategies.

Commission-based compensation
A method of compensation in which financial advisors earn commissions for selling specific financial products to clients. (See also *fee-based compensation* and *fee-only compensation.*)

Cost of living adjustment (COLA)
An increase in retirement or other benefits to counteract the effects of inflation. It is usually applied annually and set by whoever oversees the retirement plan. For example, if you are receiving a pension from working for the city, that city's retirement board of trustees sets the annual COLA.

Death benefit
A one-time Social Security benefit paid to the surviving spouse or children of an eligible deceased worker.

Delayed retirement credit (DRC)

If you delay claiming your Social Security benefits beyond your full retirement age, you will earn delayed retirement credits, which increase the amount of your benefits once you begin claiming them. It works out to be about 8% more for every year you delay, up to age 70.

Dependent

This is someone you financially support and can claim as a dependent (based on the dependency test) on your tax return, such as a child or elderly parent. A spouse is not considered a dependent.

Diversification

This is the practice of spreading investments across various assets to reduce risk. Think of it as not putting all your eggs in one basket.

Dividend

Dividends are payments made by a company to its shareholders, usually from profits. They can provide a steady income stream in addition to any gains from the stock price increasing.

Early retirement age

You can start receiving Social Security retirement benefits as early as age 62. However, taking benefits early means your monthly payments will be lower than if you were to wait until your full retirement age (See *full retirement age [FRA]*.)

Earnings record

Your earnings record is a history of the wages you've earned each year, as reported to the Social Security Administration. This record is used to calculate your Social Security benefits.

Effective tax rate (average tax rate)

This is the average rate at which your income is taxed, calculated by dividing your total tax liability by your total income.

Emerging market stock

Emerging market stocks are stocks from companies in developing countries. They offer higher growth potential but come with higher risk because of economic and political instability. (See also *large cap*, *mid cap*, *small cap*, *blue chip*, *growth*, *international*, and *value stock*.)

Estimated taxes

These are quarterly tax payments made directly to the US Treasury by people who don't otherwise have enough taxes withheld from their paychecks, investment income, Social Security, etc. It also applies to many retirees who have investment income.

Exchange-traded fund (ETF)

ETFs are like mutual funds, but they trade on stock exchanges like individual stocks. This means you can buy and sell them throughout the day, and they often have lower fees than mutual funds.

Exemption

An exemption represents a specific amount you can subtract from your gross income when calculating your taxes. It reduces your taxable income. The personal exemption remains at zero dollars (eliminating the personal exemption was part of the Tax Cuts and Jobs Act of 2017).

Expense ratio

The expense ratio is the annual fee that mutual funds or ETFs charge their shareholders, expressed as a percentage of the fund's average assets. Lower is usually better.

Extra Help Program (Low-Income Subsidy)

A program to help people with limited income and resources pay for Medicare prescription drug plan costs, such as premiums, deductibles, and copayments.

Fee-based compensation

A method of compensation that includes both fees paid by the client and commissions earned from selling financial products. (See also *commission-based compensation* and *fee-only compensation.*)

Fee-only compensation

A method of compensation in which a financial advisor is paid directly by the client for their services and does not receive commissions or other compensation from product sales. (See also *commission-based compensation* and *fee-based compensation.*)

Fiduciary

A person or organization that acts on behalf of another person or persons to manage assets. Fiduciaries are bound ethically and legally to act in the best interests of their clients.

Filing status

This determines the rate at which your income is taxed and your eligibility for certain deductions and credits. The main statuses are *single*, *married filing jointly*, *married filing separately*, *head of household*, and *qualifying widow(er)*.

Formulary

A list of prescription drugs covered by a Medicare Part D plan or a Medicare Advantage plan that includes drug coverage. The list is created by the insurance company and can vary from plan to plan.

Full retirement age (FRA)

The age at which you become eligible to receive your full Social Security retirement benefits. This age varies depending on the year you were born, typically between 65 and 67.

Government pension offset (GPO)
GPO can reduce your Social Security spousal or survivor benefits if you receive a pension from a government job not covered by Social Security.

Gross income
This is the total income you receive from all sources before any taxes or other deductions. It includes wages, interest, dividends, rental income, and other earnings.

Growth stock
Growth stocks are shares in companies expected to grow at an above-average rate compared to other companies. They often don't pay dividends, since the companies reinvest profits to fuel further growth. (See also *large cap*, *mid cap*, *small cap*, *blue chip*, *emerging market*, *international*, and *value stock*.)

Hedging
A strategy used to offset potential losses in one investment by making another investment that moves differently. It's like an insurance policy for your portfolio.

High-yield bond
Also known as *junk bond* (but it sounds better to call it high yield). These are bonds with lower credit ratings but that offer higher interest rates to compensate for the increased risk of default.

I bond
I bonds are US government savings bonds that earn interest based on combining a fixed rate and an inflation rate. They are designed to protect your investment from inflation.

Inflation

The rate at which the general level of prices for goods and services rises, thereby eroding purchasing power. On a practical level, retirees generally experience a higher rate of inflation than the average person because of their different types of purchases, such as healthcare services.

Inflation risk

This is the risk that the money you invest today won't be worth as much in the future because of rising prices. Inflation can eat into your investment returns, especially if your money is in low-yield investments.

Interest rate risk

This is the risk that changes in interest rates will affect the value of your investments, especially bonds. When interest rates rise, bond prices typically fall and vice versa.

International stock

International stocks are shares in companies based outside your home country (for most people reading this book, the US). They can add sound diversification to your portfolio but also come with currency and political risks. (See also *large cap*, *mid cap*, *small cap*, *blue chip*, *emerging market*, *growth*, and *value stock.*)

Individual retirement account (IRA)

IRAs are individual retirement arrangements that allow saving for retirement with certain tax advantages. Types include traditional, Roth, SEP, simple, and SARSEP.

Itemized deduction

These are specific expenses you can deduct from your adjusted gross income, such as medical expenses, mortgage interest, and charitable contributions. Taxpayers typically choose to itemize if the total is greater than the standard deduction.

Joint life option

A retirement pension payment option that provides benefits for the lifetimes of both the retiree and a designated beneficiary, often the retiree's spouse. (See also *single life option* and *period certain option*.)

Large cap stock

Large cap stocks are shares in large, established companies with market capitalizations typically over $10 billion. They are generally considered more stable but might offer lower growth potential than a small cap stock. (See also *mid cap*, *small cap*, *blue chip*, *emerging market*, *growth*, *international*, and *value stock*.)

Life expectancy

The average number of additional years a person is expected to live based on statistical averages.

Lifetime earnings

These are the total earnings over your working life that have been subject to Social Security taxes. Your lifetime earnings are used to calculate your benefits.

Liquidity

Liquidity refers to how easily an asset can be converted into cash without affecting its price. Stocks are generally very liquid, while real estate is not so much.

Longevity risk

This is a risk that you'll live longer than you expect. You may not call this a risk at first, but consider what might happen if your money doesn't last as long as you do.

Marginal tax bracket

This refers to the tax rate you pay on your last dollar of income. The

US tax system is progressive, so as your income increases, the rate of tax on additional income also increases.

Market capitalization
Market cap is a way to measure a company's total value. It is calculated by multiplying the number of shares a company has outstanding by its current stock price. For example, if a company has 20 million shares outstanding and a share price of $100, its market cap is $2 billion.

Market risk
Also known as *systematic risk*, this is the risk that the entire market will decline, impacting all investments. It's like being caught in a storm; it doesn't matter if you're in a fancy car or an old clunker, you're going to get wet. (*Unsystematic risk* is risk you can virtually eliminate through diversification.)

Maximum earnings
Each year, there is a limit on the amount of earnings subject to Social Security taxes. This is known as the maximum taxable earnings. For example, in 2025, the maximum was $176,100.

Medicaid
Medicaid is a joint federal and state program that helps with medical costs for people with limited income and resources. Some people qualify for both Medicare and Medicaid (known as *dual eligibility*).

Medicare
Medicare is a federal health insurance program primarily for people aged 65 or older, but it also covers certain younger individuals with disabilities and people with end-stage renal disease. Various "parts" help cover hospital stays, medical services, and prescription drugs.

Medicare Advantage plans

Also referred to as Medicare Part C, these are health plans offered by private companies that provide all Part A and Part B benefits. They often include extra benefits such as prescription drug coverage, dental care, and vision care.

Medicare Part A

This part of Medicare covers inpatient hospital care and, for a limited time, skilled nursing facility care, hospice, and some home healthcare. Most people don't pay a premium for Part A if they or their spouse paid Medicare taxes while working.

Medicare Part B

Medicare Part B covers outpatient care, doctors' services, preventive services, and some home healthcare. It requires a monthly premium, which varies based on one's income.

Medicare Part C

See *Medicare Advantage plans.*

Medicare Part D

This part of Medicare provides prescription drug coverage. Part D plans are offered by private insurance companies and can be added to original Medicare (Parts A and B) or included in Medicare Advantage plans (Part C).

Medicare Savings Program (MSP)

A program that helps people with limited income and resources pay Medicare premiums, deductibles, coinsurance, and copayments. There are several types of MSPs, including the Qualified Medicare Beneficiary Program and the Specified Low-Income Medicare Beneficiary Program.

Medicare supplement plans (Medigap)

These plans help pay some of the healthcare costs that original Medicare doesn't cover, such as copayments, coinsurance, and deductibles. They do not cover prescription drugs. They are sold by private companies and are different from Medicare Advantage plans. Medigap plans come in several standardized plan types, labeled A, B, C, D, F, G, K, L, M, and N. Each plan offers a different set of benefits, but plans of the same letter provide the same coverage no matter which company sells them.

Medigap

See *Medicare supplement plans.*

Mid cap stock

Mid cap stocks are neither large nor small cap; they're middle, or "mid." Mid cap companies have a market capitalization between $2 billion and $10 billion. They are generally considered more stable than small caps but less stable than large caps. (See also *large cap*, *small cap*, *blue chip*, *emerging market*, *growth*, *international*, and *value stock.*)

Modern portfolio theory (MPT)

MPT is a theory that suggests how investors can build portfolios to maximize expected return based on a given level of market risk. It emphasizes diversification of various asset classes to reduce risk.

Municipal bond

Municipal bonds are bonds issued by local governments or agencies. The interest earned on municipal bonds is often exempt from federal (and sometimes state and local) taxes, making them attractive for some investors. They generally pay a lower interest rate compared to taxable bonds, all things being equal.

Mutual fund

Think of mutual funds as a big pot of money collected from many investors. This pot is then used to buy a variety of stocks, bonds, or other securities. It's managed by a professional, which is great if you prefer to leave the investment decisions to someone else.

Old-Age, Survivors, and Disability Insurance (OASDI)

OASDI is the official name for Social Security benefits, covering retirement, survivor, and disability benefits.

Pension

A retirement plan that provides a fixed monthly income (or a one-time lump sum payment) to employees who have retired after reaching a certain age and meeting specific service requirements. Pensions are typically funded by employers, which may include private companies, government entities, etc.

Period certain option

A retirement pension payment option that provides benefits for a specified period of time, regardless of whether the retiree is alive. If the retiree dies before the period ends, payments continue to a beneficiary for the remainder of the period. (See also *single life option* and *joint life option*.)

Portfolio

The collection of investments you own. A well-balanced portfolio typically includes a mix of asset types to manage risk and return.

Preferred stock

A type of stock that gives holders preferential treatment in dividends and asset liquidation but usually doesn't come with voting rights. It's like a hybrid of a stock and a bond.

Premature withdrawal penalty

A penalty imposed by the IRS on withdrawals taken from a retirement account before a certain age. For example, for traditional IRAs, it's age 59½. Typically, this penalty is 10% of the amount withdrawn, in addition to any regular income taxes owed.

Pre-tax investments

These are investments made with income that hasn't yet been taxed, such as contributions to a traditional IRA or 401(k). You pay taxes on these funds when you withdraw them in retirement.

Preventive services

Medicare covers various preventive services to help you stay healthy and detect health problems early. These services include screenings, vaccinations, and annual wellness visits.

Primary insurance amount (PIA)

PIA is the amount you will receive in Social Security benefits if you retire at your full retirement age. It's based on your average indexed monthly earnings (AIME).

Quarters of coverage

To qualify for Social Security benefits, you need to earn a certain number of quarters (i.e., three-month periods) of coverage. A quarter of coverage is earned by working and paying Social Security taxes on your earnings. Generally, you need 40 quarters (or ten years of work) to be eligible for retirement benefits.

Risk tolerance

This is your ability and willingness to endure market fluctuations and losses. It's an essential factor in determining your investment strategy.

Robo-advisor

A robo-advisor is an automated platform that provides financial advice or investment management with minimal human supervision, often using algorithms.

Roth 401(k)

A type of 401(k) retirement savings plan that allows employees to contribute after-tax dollars. Qualified distributions in retirement are tax-free. (See also *401(k)*.)

Roth 403(b)

Similar to a Roth 401(k), this is a retirement savings plan for employees of public schools and certain nonprofit organizations. Contributions are made with after-tax dollars, and qualified distributions are tax-free. (See also *403(b)*.)

Roth individual retirement account (IRA)

An IRA allowing a person to set aside after-tax income up to a specified amount each year. If the account is at least five years old and withdrawals are after age 59½ all withdrawals are tax- and penalty-free.

Single life option

A retirement pension payment option that provides benefits for the retiree's lifetime but does not continue to a spouse or other beneficiary after the retiree's death. (See also *joint life option* and *period certain option*.)

Skilled nursing facility (SNF)

An SNF provides high-level medical care and rehabilitation services to patients who don't need hospital care but can't be cared for at home. Medicare Part A covers limited stays in SNFs following a hospital stay.

Small cap stock

Small cap stocks are shares in smaller companies with market capitalizations between $300 million and $2 billion. They often have higher growth potential but come with higher risk. (See also *large cap*, *mid cap*, *blue chip*, *emerging market*, *growth*, *international*, and *value stock*.)

Social Security

Social Security is a US government program that provides financial support to eligible retirees, disabled individuals, and their families. It's funded through payroll taxes and helps ensure that people have income during retirement, after a disability, or in case of a family breadwinner's death.

Social Security benefits

These are the monthly payments you receive from the Social Security Administration upon retirement ("retirement"), disability ("disability"), or after the death of a family breadwinner ("survivor").

Social Security computation years

These are the years used to calculate your Social Security benefits. For retirement benefits, the computation years are the highest 35 years of your earnings.

Social Security credit

Credits are earned based on your work and the Social Security taxes you pay. You need a certain number of credits to qualify for benefits. In 2025, for example, you could earn one credit for every $1,810 in earnings, up to four credits per year.

Social Security reduced benefits

If you start receiving Social Security retirement benefits before your full retirement age, your benefits will be reduced. This reduction is often permanent, unless you use the 12-month exception.

Special minimum benefit

A minimum benefit amount for individuals who have worked for many years but have had low earnings. This ensures they receive a slightly higher benefit than the regular calculation would provide.

Standard deduction

This is a flat amount that reduces your taxable income. The amount varies based on your filing status. You choose to use the standard deduction if the total of your itemized deductions is less than the standard deduction.

Stock

When you buy a stock, you're purchasing a small piece of ownership in a company. Stocks can make you money through price appreciation (the stock's price goes up) or dividends (receiving a share of the company's profits). (See also *large cap*, *mid cap*, *small cap*, *blue chip*, *emerging market*, *growth*, *international*, and *value stock*.)

Supplemental Security Income (SSI)

SSI is a program that provides financial assistance to individuals with low income and limited resources, including those who are elderly, blind, or disabled. SSI is funded by general tax revenues, not Social Security taxes.

Systematic risk

See *market risk.*

Systemic risk

Systemic risk is the risk that "too-big-to-fail" companies run into financial problems, which in turn causes severe instability in the industry or, worse, the entire economy. Systemic risk was a major contributor to the 2008 financial crisis.

Tax credit

Tax credits directly reduce the amount of tax you owe, dollar for dollar. Examples include the Child Tax Credit and the Earned Income Tax Credit.

Tax deduction

Tax deductions reduce your taxable income. There are two types: standard deduction and itemized deductions. Common itemized deductions include mortgage interest, state and local taxes, and charitable contributions. Taxpayers typically choose to take the higher of the standard deduction or the total of itemized deductions.

Tax evasion

Illegally avoiding paying taxes, typically by not reporting all income or by claiming false deductions. It's a serious crime; don't do it.

Tax-sheltered annuities (TSAs)

Retirement plans that allow employees of certain nonprofit organizations and public schools to invest pre-tax dollars in annuities that grow tax-deferred until retirement.

Tax strategies

These are plans and actions you can take to reduce your taxable income, such as contributing to a retirement plan or taking advantage of tax credits.

Taxable income

This is the amount of your income that is subject to income tax (i.e., your adjusted gross income minus any deductions, standard or itemized).

Tax-deferred
This means you can delay paying taxes on certain income until a later date, typically when you withdraw funds from retirement accounts such as a 401(k) or IRA.

Tax-free income
This is income that is not subject to tax, such as interest from municipal bonds or gifts.

Traditional individual retirement account (IRA)
An IRA in which contributions, up to a specified amount each year, are generally tax-deductible and withdrawals during retirement are taxed as ordinary income.

Value stock
Value stocks are shares of companies that appear to be undervalued based on their fundamentals, such as low price-to-earnings ratios. Investors buy them hoping their true value will be recognized by the market over time. (See also *large cap*, *mid cap*, *small cap*, *blue chip*, *emerging market*, *growth*, and *international stock.*)

W-2 form
This IRS form reports your annual wages and the amount of taxes withheld from your paycheck. Employers provide it to employees and the IRS.

Withholding
This is the amount of federal income tax withheld from your paycheck by your employer and sent to the IRS on your behalf.

Yield
Yield is the income return on an investment, such as interest or dividends, expressed as a percentage of the investment's cost.

Acknowledgments

There are so many who helped me with this book.

Pati, my wife. The most positive, upbeat, and energetic person I know. She loves me in spite of my many imperfections.

Dennis Crean, a great editor with insightful suggestions. He has made this book not only better but also, I must admit, readable.

Heather Misialek, my personal assistant and all-time amazing person. She thinks what I think before I think it. My work and personal lives are better because of her.

Carol Ringrose Alexander, CFP®, an outstanding retirement advisor and colleague. She read several chapters and shared her feedback. Through the years, she has helped me improve my writing by sharing her own extensive writing experience.

Brenda Bolander, CPA, CFP®, another expert retirement financial advisor who shared her thoughts on many chapters. She loves her job, and it shows.

Sylvia Sterling, CFP®, an expert retirement financial advisor whom I often turn to with the toughest retirement questions. She looked over several chapters and shared her thoughts.

Jimmy J. Williams, CPA, CFP®, who read the complete manuscript for technical errors. He wrote the foreword to my book *The*

All-Weather Retirement Portfolio and is a co-speaker with me at many AICPA Advanced Personal Financial Planning conferences. I helped Jimmy get started in the business, and he has helped me get better ever since then.

Theodore J. Sarenski, CPA/PFS™, CFP®, is the chief executive officer and president of Blue Ocean Strategic Capital. He is a nationally known speaker and writer on Social Security. Ted read my chapter on Social Security and made great suggestions.

And to the many others not named here—including the hundreds of clients who've been asking me questions over all the years—my deepest thanks to you, too. I quite literally couldn't have written this book without you!

About the Author

Randy L. Thurman started in the financial planning business in 1986. As a result of 40 years of dedication and commitment to excellence in financial planning, Randy is frequently lauded as one of the nation's most trusted investment advisors. He specializes in helping those who have retired (or are about to retire) have a comfortable income for life.

He is a certified public accountant (CPA) and a Certified Financial Planner® professional, also known as a CFP® professional. He holds the Personal Financial Specialist™ (PFS™) credential, which recognizes CPAs who have additional experience and expertise in financial planning. Randy holds four academic degrees, including a BS in electrical engineering and an MBA from Oklahoma State University, and has taught investing, personal finance, and economics at the college level.

In 1990, Randy founded the firm Financial Planning Company of Oklahoma, which, in 1997, merged with Retirement Investment Advisors, Inc. He continues today as chief executive officer. Under his leadership, the firm has become one of the largest fee-only investment advisory firms in Oklahoma, with over $1.2 billion in assets under management. All the advisors of the firm are CFP® professionals and/or CPA/PFS™.

Over the years, Randy has shared his expertise and insight as the author of seven books and an extensive list of articles on financial planning, investing, and business ethics. His book *The All-Weather Retirement Portfolio: Your Post-Retirement Investment Guide to a Worry-Free Income for Life* provides time-tested guidance for financial peace of mind, while *One More Step: 638 Quotations for Runners to Entertain and Inspire You* inspires runners and others to realize their goals. His articles have appeared in *CPA Focus*, *Medical Economics*, *NW Style Magazine*, *405 Magazine*, *Metro Journal*, *The Oklahoman*, and others.[34] He is much sought after as a speaker for conferences, workshops, and broadcast media, including appearances on Fox News Channel's *Fox on Money* and as the former host of the weekly radio program *Money Talks*.

Randy is also active as a volunteer in his community. He is a member of the South Oklahoma City Rotary Club, sits on boards, and serves as an investment consultant for nonprofit organizations, including the Investment Committee of the YMCA of Greater Oklahoma City, the Oklahoma City Community College Foundation, the Oklahoma Society of CPAs, and the Oklahoma City Employee Retirement System. Randy has also been recognized at the local level for excellence and leadership, including:

- South Oklahoma City Citizen of the Year
- OSCPA Accounting Hall of Fame
- Oklahoma Business Ethics Compass Award
- Oklahoma Society of CPAs Award for Outstanding CPA in Financial Planning
- *The Journal Record* Beacon Award, Charitable Influence: Small Business

34 A complete and up-to-date list, including criteria, is available upon request.

- *The Journal Record* 2021 Power List: The Thirty Most Influential People in Banking and Finance

Most importantly, Randy is a family man who treasures time with his wife and son. He's an active member of his church community and an enthusiastic reader, writer, and pickleball player.

For more information about Randy L. Thurman's work and to contact him, visit randylthurman.com.

Also by Randy L. Thurman

The All-Weather Retirement Portfolio: Your Post-Retirement Investment Guide to a Worry-Free Income for Life

Five Steps to Finding a Financial Advisor You Can Trust

The Worry-Free Retirement Guide to Finding a Trustworthy Financial Advisor

More Than a Millionaire: Your Path to Wealth, Happiness, and a Purposeful Life—Starting Now!

One More Step: 638 Quotations for Runners to Entertain and Inspire You

Two More Steps: 638 More Quotations for Runners to Make You Laugh and Lace Up Your Shoes

Get Rich Slowly … but Surely!

The Richest Man in Babylon: The Easy-to-Read Edition (by George Clason, completely edited and rewritten by Randy L. Thurman)

Index

F

G

H

I

J

L

M

N

O

P

T

U

V

W

www.ingramcontent.com/pod-product-compliance
Lightning Source LLC
LaVergne TN
LVHW040412240526
839547LV00003B/19

* 9 7 9 8 8 9 1 8 8 3 8 9 5 *